# INSIDE THE MIND OF A CONQUEROR

Conquering the Obstacles in Your Mind
Winning the Battle in Reality

## WAYNE BILLY, JR.

HOUSE CAPACITY PUBLISHING
DETROIT

# Inside the Mind of a Conqueror

Inside the Mind of a Conqueror
Copyright © 2017 by Wayne Billy, Jr.

Scripture quotations are from the KJV® Bible (The Holy Bible, King James Version®), copyright © 2001 by Crossway, a publishing ministry of Good News Publishers. Used by permission. All rights reserved.

**Inside the Mind of a Conqueror**
Copyright © 2017 by Wayne Billy, Jr.
Published by House Capacity Publishing
Detroit, MI
www.housecapacity.com

All rights reserved. No part of this publication may be reproduced, distributed, or transmitted in any form or by any means, including photocopying, recording, or other electronic or mechanical methods, without the prior written permission of the publisher, except in the case of brief quotations embodied in critical reviews and certain other noncommercial uses permitted by copyright law. For permission requests, write to the publisher, addressed "Attention: Permissions Coordinator," at housecapacity@gmail.com.

For booking and purchasing information please visit www.housecapacity.com
ISBN-10: 0692955011
ISBN-13: 978-0692955017

Photography and graphic design by Timothy Paule II

## DEDICATION

*I dedicate this book to those who feel abandoned, lost, alone, or feel like they don't have the strength to be conquerors. I dedicate this book to the young man who doesn't have that father figure or role model in his life, who feels like all odds are against him. To the young lady who's been abused not just physically but mentally and emotionally and she feels broken on the inside. To the young fathers who are facing battles of being leaders to their families. To the young single mothers who are struggling doing both roles. I dedicate this book to those who are broken, lost and confused. To those who feel like giving up, and to those who have been in obstacles that almost caused you to lose your life. I dedicate this to those who are facing obstacles and battles and it seems like it's impossible to conquer. If any of these describe you, this book is for you.*

Inside the Mind of a Conqueror

# CONTENTS

|   | | |
|---|---|---|
|   | Foreword by Kierra C. Jones | 7 |
|   | Introduction | 11 |
| 1 | "Elena" | 15 |
| 2 | In Custody | 29 |
| 3 | "Deacon D" | 45 |
| 4 | The Actions of Thinking | 59 |
| 5 | "Pops" | 73 |
| 6 | Homeless and Helpless | 85 |
| 7 | Battle Stage of the Mind | 95 |
| 8 | The Aftermath of Thinking | 105 |
| 9 | Repent, Release, Receive and Rebuild | 117 |
| 10 | Conquer What's Conquering You | 125 |
| 11 | Restored and Reloaded | 137 |

# FOREWORD

I READ MANY OF MY BOOKS LIKE I WATCH movies. If a movie has been written well and it evokes some type of emotion from me, honey, you're going to hear me! I'm going to talk back to it if it's good. In the same manner, I found myself having an ongoing conversation with Wayne Billy, Jr.'s *Inside the Mind of a Conqueror*. His story drew me in and made me an instant advocate of his victory. I found myself being angry with him, but also having compassion and hope for his future. I found myself reacting with the same type of emotions that he had displayed as he took blow by blow and experienced trial after trial.

I am so glad that God has given Wayne the gift of ministry and evangelism because I truly believe that he is called to reach the masses. I believe that God has given him an out-the-box ministry that extends well beyond the four walls of the church. As a peer, I can honestly say that this generation needs his message, his voice, and his testimony. There are people currently in situations that have overtaken them, and this book is the message of hope that they need.

When you read this book, don't just read it to get the inside scoop on this man and his different family conflicts. That's messy and that's not the point of the book. Instead, glean from it the lessons and nuggets that Wayne had to learn to truly become a conqueror. Everyone won't experience the things that Wayne has, but everyone will face battles and obstacles. What will be your response? What will be your position?

I admire Wayne for having the courage to write such a story and revisit one of the most difficult times in his life. I appreciate his vulnerability and transparency; I admonish the reader to also do the same. I also commend Wayne for having the discipline to put his thoughts to paper, trust God, and finish his first book. As a colleague, I understand how massive such an accomplishment is. Welcome to the club, Billy!

I have one more request to you as a reader—apply the principles that he is sharing! Don't just read past them, take the time to pray and truly experience God's presence as you interact with these pages. Talk back to the book if you need to! Most importantly, make up in your mind to be better once you have finished. Allow the Holy Spirit to minister to you through Wayne's story, and decide to move forward as a conqueror. Decide to no longer allow satan to have control over your thoughts, and decide that victory shall always be your mantra.

Thank you, Wayne, for sharing such an amazing message of resiliency and strength. I am excited about where God is taking you and who you will become as a result of that journey.

Kierra C. Jones, author
*The Power of the Panties*
*I'm So Over It*

Inside the Mind of a Conqueror

# INTRO

How do we conquer or overcome the challenges and obstacles that we face on a day to day basis? How do we conquer the very thing that was set up to destroy us, to distract us, or even confuse us? How do we handle pain, suffering, betrayal, peer pressure, depression, or guilt? What do we do when we done all we can and still we get no results? How do we handle death within our personal lives? What steps do we take to mend the broken hearts, to break and conquer generational curses and soul-ties? How can we be a good example or inspiration to those who are around us and are looking up to us?

These are some of the questions that we ask ourselves probably every day. Our mind is where questions are birthed, dreams are shown, and ideas are created. It is also a place where addictions, bad habits, guilt and the past haunts and dwells. Our minds, or our thinking is what controls our five senses: seeing, hearing, smelling, tasting, and touching. Our thinking controls what we say or do in life, and it births our opinions when it comes down to debating, creating, or decision making. It's a place where God will speak and communicate with us, but it is also a place where Satan speaks and attacks with fear, hate, and corruption. How? Because our thinking regulates us. Sometimes we ask the questions "How do we conquer what's coming against us, or what do we do when we come face to face with battles and obstacles in our lives? How can we conquer what we don't understand or cannot see?"

In the Bible, Ephesians 6:12 says,

*"For we wrestle not against flesh and blood, but against principalities, against powers, against the rulers of the darkness of this world, against spiritual wickedness in high places."*

Everything that we go through or have an encounter with does affect us naturally, but it can also affect us spiritually. If we allow ungodly thoughts to take residence in our minds, those thoughts can destroy us. What does that statement mean? Here is an example: if you put your trust in someone, whether he or she is a friend or a person you are in a relationship with, and that person betrays that trust, the hurt you experience will target your thinking. It can cause you to look, act or think differently about that person. Of if a spouse cheats on their companion, the hurt and the pain will target their thinking and will cause them to lose trust or interest in that person and will begin to look for ways to ending the relationship. That's the natural, but spiritually it will cause you to be blind. Sometimes we allow ourselves to get into situations and we think we know the outcome of it, but naturally if it turns out bad, we wouldn't know how to handle it. Spiritually, God will warn us before, then he will give us the strength and guidance to go through and handle it the right way. How? The only way God can do that is when we humble ourselves, seek his face and live for him. Spend time with him by reading and meditating on his word, praying and fasting. Once we do these things, God will begin to equip us with the helmet of salvation, so that his word can and will stick within our minds.

What is the helmet of salvation? The helmet of salvation is the fifth piece of God's armor that's represented by the Roman soldier's helmet. Without this helmet it would be impossible to enter and win battles. The purpose of the helmet is to protect the head from mental injury or warfare that we might face on a day to day basis. The helmet of salvation also helps us meditate on God's word, and it will allow God to regulate and guard our thoughts.

*"When we don't guard our mind, it becomes a target."*

What do we think about on day to day basis or when we are laying in our beds at night? What are we birthing in our minds and thoughts? How do we handle not just the positive thoughts, but the negative thoughts? Sometimes we can't figure out how to handle different types of obstacles and situations in our mind, or the battles that come into our lives. Sometimes we leave those battles unresolved and it becomes a target for a direct attack.

# CHAPTER 1

## *"Elena"*

I WAS SITTING ON MY MOTHER'S PORCH, TREMBLING and crying—I was attempting to medicate myself with the bottle of alcohol I had brought home with me from prom the night before. I watched the rain water replenish the earth, and couldn't help but think that, unlike the rain which had a specific assignment and function, my life had no meaning or purpose. I felt disposable and that no one else in the world had any regard for me. Earlier, I had received a text from my girlfriend saying that she didn't want to be with me anymore. I called her and asked her why, and she told me that my mother called her cussing her out because I had come home from the prom too late. In my anger, I started yelling at my mom. *Why would she do such a thing? Didn't she know that my girlfriend was the only one who really cared about me?* Another person would have been able to deal with a break up and process it in a healthy way, but I couldn't. I was mentally unstable, emotionally damaged, and in spiritual duress. In my mind, nothing was going right in my life, and besides that one little glitter of joy that had decided not to be a part of my life anymore, what did I really have?

After I stared at the puddles in the street long enough, I went back inside and tip-toed around. I wanted to make sure that everyone was asleep. When I went downstairs, I saw that my little brothers weren't awake anymore, so I knew that it was the right opportunity. I started to gather sheets, cords, and other objects that I thought would be able to do the job effectively. I went to grab a chair so that I could stand on top of it and throw the cord over the light fixture. I had managed to tie a loop at the other end of the rope, measuring it out to make sure that my head could fit inside of it. I was there, on top of the chair, with the rope around my neck, when my little brother walked in.

"Wayne, what are you doing?" he panicked.

"I ain't doing nothing. Just go. You ain't seen nothin'."

He shrieked and then yelled out to my mom, "Ma, Wayne tryna kill hisself!"

I tried to hurry and step off the chair before she came because I wanted so desperately to end my life. I didn't secure the cord properly because when I stepped off the chair, my weight ended up bringing down the light fixture and some of the ceiling. My mom grabbed me and brought me upstairs. She was frantic and asked me a million times why I would try do something like that, but I didn't want to answer. I didn't want to talk to anyone. The pain that I had been experiencing had taken over my mind.

During that stage of my life, I was in a deeply depressive state, and I felt empty. I didn't have a job, I had just finished school, but I felt like I wasn't doing anything with my life. To make matters worse, all my family really did was tell me about how I wasn't doing anything productive and how much I'd "messed up". I felt like I didn't have anybody.

During my strongest feelings of depression and failure, I later met another girl we'll call "Elena". Before I met her, I had designed an image in my mind of the type of woman that I wanted. It's crazy because even though she was so young, she fit the exact description of what I wanted: long hair, light skin, green eyes. She had the exact body type that I was attracted to. She definitely didn't look her age. It didn't matter to me that she was so young—significantly younger than me actually—because I was looking at everything that I wanted in a woman. She was right before my very eyes.

Our relationship began with us just talking from time to time. Once I realized that she was pursuing me, things escalated from there. We were having conversations that really caused me to think about my life. It sounds crazy, but even at her age, she motivated me to get up and do something with myself and be something better. She gave me the extra push and motivation that I needed. When I was surrounded by people who talked down to me and dogged me out, she only had positive uplifting things to say. She brought me out of my depression. I begin to think of things in the long run with this girl; if she was able to inspire me and help me be better, what could our future together really look like?

Not to mention, she did things for me that no other girl did. She would buy me clothes, shoes, and other expensive gifts that she paid for with the money that she earned working in her family's restaurant. She wasn't legally able to work because she was underaged, but I guess her family didn't really care about that. When my birthday rolled around, she planned an entire day for me: dinner, movies, cake, and gifts. All I wanted was for somebody to appreciate me and have my back.

We didn't tell anybody that we were together for about four or five months. Eventually, I met Elena's mom and the rest of her family—cousins, aunties, everybody. They made it seem like our relationship was fine. Her mom even eased my apprehension by telling me how many years her husband had on her. She told me to just take care of Elena and treat her well and that there was nothing wrong with our relationship, as long as we were happy. Her family was so supportive of our relationship that even when I didn't have a job, her grandmother pulled some strings where she was working and got me hired! I was thinking that Elena was it. I had found the person I would spend the rest of my life with—I knew that I would probably just have to wait more than a few years to make it official.

I quickly found out that there had to be someone raising an eyebrow at Elena's and my relationship because I never got to meet her pops. They would tell me about how "cool" he was and how much we'd get along, but they always told me that I'd better leave before her pops made it in from work. I was thinking, *How is this cool if I can't meet her dad?* It definitely raised a red flag that maybe this relationship wasn't appropriate, but I was so caught up in Elena that I couldn't rationalize beyond what I felt for her, how beautiful she was, and how she had really been a light in my darkness.

When I brought Elena up to my brother and my older sister, they really didn't have much to say. They did mention how "grown" she looked, but nobody really told me to try to steer clear of her. My family had the mentality of, "That's your life. You do what you do. That's your business." Everybody else was dismissing the relationship, but when I brought Elena up to my mom, she clearly told me to leave her alone. I insisted that Elena didn't even look her age, but my mother starkly corrected me and told me that what she looked like didn't matter. She specifically told me to break it off and stay away from Elena.

I didn't listen. Part of the reason why I didn't listen to her is because I felt that my family had spent so much time discouraging me and trying to control me. I didn't want my mother to attempt to put her foot on my neck again and tell me to abandon the only person who seemed to genuinely care for me, so, I discarded her advice. I looked at all that I had going for myself now: a job, a beautiful "woman", and road to a great future. I was the man.

Eventually, my relationship with Elena progressed even further, and we started to have sex. So for about two years, we were together like we had a full relationship. She would buy me expensive watches and jewelry and everything; I would buy things for her and take her out. She was the best girlfriend I'd had. The bond I felt with her was so strong that I blocked out every bit of sound reasoning that I had. A soul tie was birthed because I found myself doing things for her and connecting with her on different levels that I never thought I would connect with any other woman. It's like an emptiness or a void was filled that I didn't know existed. It was like I was on this high that I never wanted to come down from.

While I was in this situation, I thought I had it all. I was in college, I attended ITT Tech, I was taking up computer engineering, I had a job working at Target during the holiday season, and plus the woman that I created in my thoughts was made in reality. I didn't realize that satan had my mind in fantasy island and it was all set up for my destruction. My family continued to warn me, but I ignored the signs because I always thought that my family belittled me anyway. The soul tie I had with Elena grew stronger, and I was satisfied with my life. I became very prideful, and then my thoughts became centered around proving that I was nothing that my family said I was. I wanted them to know that I had come up despite their many shots against me. I wanted them to see that I was successful—without their help. I wanted them to respect me.

Everything seemed to be all bright and sunny in our relationship until Elena told me that she was really sick. At first, her family just brushed it off and assured me that she would be better in no time. There was one particular day when Elena didn't want to get out of bed and do anything. It seemed like her condition was getting worse. I couldn't allow myself to just watch her suffer while she was sick, so I advised her to go to the hospital. I didn't realize that her hospital visit would be the door opener to my down fall. I remember sitting in a classroom in college and getting a text that almost destroyed me: "I'm pregnant." Honestly no words, or thinking was being developed because I was beyond scared.

*What would this mean for Elena and me? Was I even ready to be a father? Was she even old enough to be a good mother? How would she finish school? What would either of our parents say?*

At three a.m. I got a text from Elena saying that she was sorry. I was confused because I didn't know why she was sorry—I mean, it took both of us to make a baby. Her pops still had no idea that I existed. For two years I had been ducking and dodging him because her family didn't know the "right time" to tell him about me. I got to the point where I really wanted to meet him because I was so in love with his daughter, but it never happened. If I came over to visit, I still had to be out of their house before two o'clock. So imagine what he must have felt discovering that his baby girl was pregnant, not even knowing that she was even sexually active. Imagine what he must have felt after finding out that a *grown man* had impregnated his daughter. Then another text came in saying that her father had just found out and that things were about to get worse.

Now my thoughts became mixed, and my vision became blurry. I didn't know what would happen next. It kind of felt like I was wandering in the wilderness with no food, no water and no strategy. I got on my knees, but I couldn't speak a prayer. I couldn't figure out why. Understand that when you have a prideful spirit, you're going in the direction of destruction. When you operate outside of the will of God, sometimes God's hedge of protection is removed. You could lose everything. In this case, I didn't even know that God had removed his protection. We were then faced with a sobering consequence: either I had to go to jail or she was going to get taken away from her family. The question I had on my mind was when either of these would happen.

I told my mom that Elena was pregnant, and it really was the first time in a long time that I was looking for her to tell me what to do. I didn't know what was getting ready to happen, and I wasn't sure that I was ready for it either. I felt ashamed because I knew that if I had just listened to my mom when she told me to leave Elena alone that I probably wouldn't have been in this situation in the first place. I could've prevented all of this from happening.

Sometimes the enemy can consume our mind and thinking and have us wandering on a path that feels good but is not good. Our faulty thinking can also lead us in a direction that doesn't even lead to a favorable destination. I'll never forget when it all happened—sometimes the thoughts pop up from time to time in my mind today.

After I found out that Elena was pregnant, I really didn't see her that much. Then I got a call from a detective saying that he wanted to investigate the relationship that I had with Elena. I figured that her dad must've pressed charges against me, but I didn't really know what that would mean for me. I had never really had any dealings with the police before—I mean, I was a fairly good kid—so if a detective told me that he wanted to talk to me, I just thought it meant just that. I immediately told my mom that these detectives wanted to talk to me, and I begged her to tell me what to do.

*Did I need an attorney? What was going on?* Since I had never had any run-ins with the law before this situation, I didn't really have any knowledge of my rights either. The detectives wanted me to meet them at some location, but my mom wanted them to talk to me at the house instead. It's funny how I didn't listen to any of her advice before, but when those detectives tried to big body me and intimidate me, I did everything she said.

They came to the house and they told me about all the lies that Elena had told them about our relationship. Looking back, I don't know if she even said those things, but I was so shook by the whole situation that I didn't know who or what to believe. I just broke down. They made it seem like I was just this awful guy who took advantage of this young girl, but I wasn't. Everything was consensual. Her family made it seem like it was okay. I was ignorant of what statutory rape was, so I hadn't even considered that what we had would potentially label me as a sex offender. I was just in an emotional and broken place that didn't allow me to make a wise decision regarding her. I allowed my feelings and my pride to cause me to make a stupid decision that would later on threaten my freedom.

The detectives told me to stay away from Elena until the investigation died down. I told my mom that I might have too much free time on my hands, so I got another job. I needed to occupy myself so that I could have less time to think about her and the mess I had gotten myself into. I even made up my mind to focus better in school so that I could get my engineering degree. I eventually got called for an interview with KFC and they hired me. Things were looking up, and I was able to still remain positive and stay busy while all of this was going down.

Even though I tried to stay away from Elena, she was still pulling on me. She tried to find ways to see me even though we both were told to stay away from each other. She would call my phone all the time asking when and where we could meet, but I would tell her that it wasn't a good idea for us to be seen in public with each other. Eventually, I gave in, and I would meet her at her bus stop to walk her home from school. One particular day when I was walking her home, I kept seeing a white truck that seemed to be following us. I asked Elena if she knew the people in the truck and she said that she didn't recognize anyone. Neither of us knew who it was, but it was actually one of the detectives watching us to make sure that we were not spending time with each other.

That night, I got a call from one of the detectives asking me why I had been consistently meeting Elena at her bus stop. I tried to play dumb and act like I didn't know what he was talking about. The detective, furious at this point, told me how they had someone watching us and that he knew that I had been with her. Then, I found myself panicking, so I told them that Elena's mom had asked me to pick her up.

"That's not the point!" I remember the detective screaming. "We told you not to see her and you did it anyway. I'm tired of talking now," the detective threatened.

I didn't know what was going to happen. I was so nervous. I knew I had messed up, and now I was trying to think of way to get out of this. If ever I needed God to intervene for me, it was then, but I felt that I had gone so far out of his will that he wouldn't.

# CHAPTER II

## *In Custody*

I WAS SITTING IN THE HOUSE, AND THEN I decided to resume some sort of normalcy by washing dishes. I was trying my best to forget about everything that was happening regarding Elena and the threatening words of the detective. Soon after, my daydreaming was interrupted by the sound of the police knocking at my door. We asked them why they had come to our house, and one officer responded that they had received a call about a fight in the area. My mom had actually called the police because my brother had gotten into a fight earlier that day. We were explaining the situation to the officers, but one cut me off abruptly and asked for my name.

"Me?" I answered naively, "Oh I'm his older brother, Wayne Billy, Jr."

The officer stepped away to speak to someone on his walkie-talkie, and then I heard two terrifying condemning words, "Get 'em." I was shocked because I had no idea what I did wrong and why they were told to arrest me. My brother came to my defense, telling the officers that I didn't do anything and that he was the one who had gotten into the fight. They told me that there was a warrant out for my arrest, and still, I was confused.

They placed me into handcuffs, and as soon as the cuffs clicked, it clicked in my head why they had come for me. I slipped up. The Elena situation. I was getting my just due for ignoring the warnings of the detectives. They arrested my brother, too—I guess they wanted to bring him in for questioning, but my brother was very hostile, insisting that I didn't do anything wrong. My mother was at work at the time, so we were there being arrested while my little sisters were crying in horror. I tried to console them by telling them that everything would be all right, but honestly, I didn't know.

They took my brother and me to two different buildings—I guess they didn't want us to try to conspire? I was so nervous and confused; I had no idea what was getting ready to happen to me. In any case, my mom was notified that we had been taken in, so she tried to make some sort of arrangement to have my pops come see about me while she went to figure out the situation with my brother. My father said no. Just like that. My *father* wouldn't come to the police station to inquire about his own son's arrest. That hurt me deeply.

While my mother went to go and investigate my brother's situation, I was alone. I was so nervous and shaking so much that it was hard to get my fingerprints on file. I had no idea what to expect, and I didn't know what would end up happening to me here. After they finished processing me, they put me in a holding cell. It was a long, narrow space, but still long enough for me to lie down in. I was just sitting there going over every decision that I had made up until this point, when I heard a voice in my head laughing and asking me *now what you gonna do? Where is your God now?* I tried my hardest not to go to sleep. I couldn't go to sleep if I wanted to because I could think about nothing else but my stupid decisions. All I could think was, *What Am I Doing Here? This ain't even me!*

When I finally dozed off, I was awakened by the sound of another dude entering the cell. He looked at me like I was getting ready to jump on him or something, but I told him that I didn't want any trouble.

He looked at me, relieved that he didn't have to fight me, and asked, "What you in for?"

I wasn't really comfortable talking to him because I didn't know him at all! Reluctantly, I told him about my romance with the underaged girl of my dreams because I figured that he might have been able to help me out or tell me what to do.

He told me what I had already been thinking, "Man, that's no reason for you to be arrested. I mean, if it was consensual and everybody was okay with it, then why would they arrest you?"

"I know, man," I sighed, relieved that somebody else could understand my point of view. Then he started rambling and talking nonsense—I realized that he was drunk and that he had no idea what he was talking about. The dude was in there for attacking the police at a party, so clearly, we were having two totally different experiences in that cell.

I decided not to confide in him any longer and thought about what I needed to do next. *Should I pray?* I was talking to myself, but every time I posed a question, there was that voice again shooting me down, *Nope ain't no point in you doing that because God's not going to listen.* I was trying to ignore the voice, but the voice was more adamant, *Why would you pray now? It's too late for that. You let your pride get in the way when you did what you did, so you're mine now.*

### Judged

The next day, I went before the judge; I walked towards him shackled and restrained like I was some type of beast or murderous fiend. As I suspected, he was charging me with statutory rape. I was red with embarrassment. He set my bond at $100,000, and once my mother heard it, I could see her almost collapse. I looked at him, ashamed of what I was putting my family through, and told him that I didn't have it. I told him that no one in my family had it. He wasn't even okay with ten percent.

There was really nothing else to discuss after I had encountered the judge, so they sent me back to another holding cell. I was just sitting there, hearing the buzz of people talking all around me, but I couldn't focus on what they were actually saying. I was watching people posting bail and leaving, but I knew that I wasn't going anywhere that day. I was wondering if my mother could put up something for collateral, but I knew that it was a long shot. One of the officers even walked over to me and asked me if I had any family members trying to work on getting me out, but I couldn't do anything but shake my head and say no. The only thing that was on my mind was Elena and the things I needed to remember like family phone numbers, and any other possible way that I could get out of this mess. I asked him what time it was, and once he told me that it was about 2:30 in the afternoon, I knew that I would probably see 2:30 in the morning, too. My mom had to go to work, so I was going to be here, at least for another day.

**Samson**

I felt so stupid, and I had to come to terms with what was happening to me. My mom told me not to get myself in this situation, but I didn't want to listen. I was thinking about everything that I've achieved, failing to realize that I forgot the one thing I needed the most: God. Because I had forsaken God and focused on the wrong things, I couldn't see or trace Him. Not because He left me, but because I walked away from Him.

It was like I was reliving the story of Sampson and

Delilah. In case you don't know about the story, in the Bible there was a man named Samson who had supernatural strength because of his connection with God. The connection was symbolized through his hair; if he were to cut it, that strength would leave him immediately. He was unstoppable and couldn't be defeated. Great kings couldn't even defeat him. No one knew his weakness, so they turned to the only person who he had the potential to be vulnerable with: his woman, Delilah.

    Sampson was romantically involved with Delilah, but she didn't have his best interest at heart. She didn't even serve God, which meant that this relationship couldn't have possibly been a good idea. Eventually, Delilah made a deal with Samson's enemies; she told them that she would help them defeat Sampson by seducing him and learning the secret of his strength. In return, she simply wanted to get paid. Long story short, Samson had spent so much time with this woman that he ended up telling her the source of his strength. Once he told her that is was his hair, he fell asleep, and Delilah cut it. Afterwards, she sent for warriors to come and arrest him. When Samson woke up, he didn't know that the power of God had left him, and he was powerless against his enemies. After subduing Samson, they shaved his hair, chained him up, blinded him, and had him walking around aimlessly in a dungeon.

So, how was Samson's situation similar to my own? Well, I was so caught up in Elena that I didn't realize that she was my Delilah. She had made a deal to keep her freedom in exchange for my captivity. I don't fully blame her for what she did, she really didn't know what she was doing. I had to come to the realization that even though she looked and acted like a full-grown woman, she was still unable to make sound decisions. She was a child. Time has allowed me to realize that, and time has also allowed me to see the situation from a more mature perspective and forgive her. Yet and still, the enemy still used her to as a tool to distract me from whatever it was that God had planned for me. I was blinded by what I thought what was love.

I went into the station wearing blue jeans and gym shoes, but then I was given a uniform to put on. *Wow. I have to wear this. I'm not a criminal!* I was shaking trying to put on the clothes that would make me look like all of the other men in the jail who had done worse offenses. But was I any better than they were? That voice in my head came back to taunt me, *Let's see how you handle this!*

**Don't Lose It**

The first night I was in jail, I couldn't sleep at all. I was just thinking of ways that I was going to survive this experience. "Wayne, you a man now," I told myself, "You have to protect yourself. Do what you have to do to defend yourself." The guys I met all asked me what I was in for, but I didn't want to talk to anybody. From what I heard about jail and prison life, people don't take too kindly to you if they think you violated a kid.

There was one dude who approached me and asked me what I had done—he could tell by the look on my face that I was defensive and afraid at the same time. "Relax," he had assured me, "I ain't even like that. You seemed like you're a good dude and that you probably just bumped your head. You don't even seem like you supposed to be in here."

I finally spoke telling this complete stranger the details of my case and voiced all of the frustration I held in, "Man, I ain't even really tryna talk to nobody. I ain't never been in jail before! I'm wet behind the ears with all of this. I don't—"

"Chill, man," he said, diffusing me. "When you go to the judge, ask for a personal bond. Tell him it was consensual and that you learned your lesson."

That seemed like a genius solution, only the next day when I asked for this personal bond, the judge denied me. I went right back to jail. I just wanted to go home. This was a nightmare.

After my meeting with the judge, I was moved to a cell that was in the highest tower in the Macomb County Jail. The smallest luxury I enjoyed was being able to open up the window to smell the fresh breeze and hear the birds chirp. I began to think about my family, wondering what they were doing at that very moment and whether or not they had given up on me. I figured that Elena had probably moved on by now, so I knew that I had to focus on myself and keep my sanity.

One of the guys who was in the tower with me noticed my frazzled disposition and said, "Aye man, you look like you about to lose it up in here."

"No, I'm not," I retorted. "Not up in *here* anyway."

"Just remember this," he shared, "Don't get comfortable in here. If you start to get comfortable then you'll start to act like the rest of these dudes up in here who don't care."

*I can't get comfortable in here.* I was so determined not to get comfortable in jail that I had gone ten days without visitors. I didn't set up the necessary paperwork to start receiving visitors because I didn't live there. I was not going to have my family and friends all up in the jailhouse like I was locked away for good!

Though I wasn't really feeling visitors, that didn't stop Macomb Country from bringing me visitors anyway. The most demeaning and humiliating thing I experienced while incarcerated was being on display as an example to different middle school groups of who not to become. They would bring the kids in for a "tour" of the jail and take the kids to our cells while explaining what we had been charged with! I felt like Harambe or something! Why not have a card displayed outside of my cell that told how much of a disgrace to society I really was? I was an incarcerated Black man being shown off like a zoo exhibit to a bunch of *white* kids. They were laughing, joking, and taunting us, and I couldn't believe that some of the other inmates weren't even as embarrassed as I was. When these obnoxious visits would happen, I would just hide my face and zone out until they were gone.

I went before the judge again, sticking to my plan of asking for a personal bond so that I could go home. I tried my best to persuade him that I wasn't a bad person and that I had learned my lesson. Denied.

This was now day 15 that I was in jail. After I had seen the judge again, they moved me to the last floor of the tower where I had already been kept. The word was that when you're on the last floor, it meant that you were either getting ready to go home soon, or you were going to prison. I had no idea what the last floor meant for me, but I was sick with the possibility of going to prison. Either I was going home after this, or life was about to get real for me.

My new cellmate was a gangly looking white guy. When he saw me, he jumped up, so I squared up just in case I was going to have to really defend myself.

"Man, I'm not even like that," he confessed. "If you're cool, I'm cool.

"I don't want no problems," I explained. "I'm just tryna get out of here. This is not my life; this is not who I am."

If I learned nothing else from this experience, I learned that I needed to humble myself. I believe that God had allowed all of this to happen so that I could really reflect on and denounce the pride that had gotten me into this situation in the first place.

I finally had visitation rights, and I saw my mom and dad—I just burst out in tears. She told me that my dad wanted to talk to me, but I was furious and didn't want to hear anything that he had to say.

"What could he possibly tell me? He didn't even come to see about me when all of this went down."

"I could tell you that I told you so!" he snapped.

"I'm not trying to hear all of that," I responded. "I'm here now."

"Well," my mother interjected, attempting to referee the situation, "I just want to tell you to focus on you and not worry about that girl. She already got a new boyfriend and everything. She doesn't care about you."

I admit, it stung for my mother to tell me all of that about Elena. I wasn't really hurt that the relationship was over, but that she didn't speak up when they were asking her about our relationship. Either way, this was all on me, so I just had to be at peace with the fact that she was a closed chapter in my book.

After that first visit with my mom, I went back to the cell trying to process the load she had dropped on me. I had a weird feeling upon returning, and that's when my cellmate offered up some advice: "Whatever you do, don't tell anybody what you're in here for. They can find a way to use it against you."

Then it clicked. I took all of my court papers and everything that had anything to do with my case, and flushed them all down the toilet. My cellmate was looking at me like I was crazy and asked me if I was okay. "I'm good, man. Just something that I need to do *right now*."

About three minutes later, some guys came rushing into my cell asking me what I was in for and started looking for my paperwork. They pat me down and completely trashed our cell. I guess they were annoyed with the fact that I hadn't been talking or trying to make friends, and they thought that they'd look for some leverage against me. When they left, my cellmate looked at me like I had another nose growing out of my face.

"Man, how did you know that they were going to do that?"

"Something just told me that I needed to throw my papers away right now. I just followed the voice."

### Jonah

The mundane routine of jail and my lack of freedom really started to get to me. I grew exhausted from each day being exactly like the previous: six a.m. wake-up, breakfast, lockdown for a few hours, lunch, lockdown again, recreation, lockdown, dinner, lockdown for the night.

*What do you do when you are beneath your own potential? How can you remain positive when there is no sign of hope in sight?* These thoughts were racing through my mind daily while I was pleading before different judges asking to be released and still remaining in jail. At this point I felt like Jonah in the Bible, who was stuck at the bottom of the ocean in the belly of a whale. I knew that God's grace was still with me because he didn't allow anything to happen to me. Sometimes God will break you down so that you realize that being stuck at the bottom is uncomfortable and that you need to make necessary changes or moves in uncomfortable situations. During this time, the thoughts of guilt and defeat were being implanted into my mind. I was haunted nightly by the regretful actions that had landed me in captivity.

There was one particular night that I couldn't sleep, so I decided to look out the small cell window. I gazed at the stars in the sky, and somehow those distant wonders made me begin to think about my family. Tears started to run down my face because I felt like I failed them. Still looking at the sky, I begin to ask God to help me, to forgive me, and to keep me because my mind was on the brink of depression. As I got on my knees and face, I begin to do the most powerful thing in the whole world: I begin to pray. I asked God to strengthen and guide me.

While I was praying, God showed me a vision of my whole family on their knees behind me with their hands on my shoulders praying for and with me. That night the scripture Psalms 30:5 came to mind, "Weeping may endure for a night, but joy comes in the morning." At that moment I begin to focus on gaining strength and peace in my thinking first, because I knew that it was my thinking that controlled and directed my actions, my attitude, and my environment. It wasn't easy, but I begin to press. As I continued to humble myself and pray, another scripture came to mind: "God will keep you in perfect peace, if you keep your mind stayed on him (Isaiah 26:3)."

There may be times when you will have depressive and guilty thoughts, or you might be on the edge of giving up and settling, but know that there is power in prayer and know that prayer is the answer. You just have to humble yourself and press in God's presence.

# CHAPTER 3

## *"Deacon D"*

THE NEXT MORNING, I FELT A LITTLE MORE revived. I knew that I had to reshape my thinking, so I decided to feed my mind the best food possible: the Word of God. I would study my Bible every day and receive a new revelation each time I opened the pages. I was so overwhelmed with knowledge that I started to take notes. Eventually, my notes became lessons and sermons that resulted from my spirit being fed. I felt a fire being lit inside of me, and I knew that it was because I had surrendered my life and my old ways to God.

My family came to visit me and there were tears of joy, because when I told them my vision of them praying with me, and how I was the edge of depression, they encouraged and motivated me. At that moment, this one power thought was planted in my mind, "If you can conquer it in your mind, you conquer it in reality." I stuck to that mantra, and I was determined to be a conqueror.

Shortly after my family came to visit, I was in my cell reading the Bible and writing lessons, and then an older guy came in. He looked at me curiously and asked me what I was writing. It was kind of strange because I hadn't really exchanged words with him before, and I don't know why he was persuaded to ask me about my leisurely activities. My defenses were always up because I really didn't know who to trust, so I didn't tell him anything. The next thing I knew, he took my notebook from me and *left*. It was crazy. I was thinking, *Who is this guy? How he just gon' take my stuff?* I wasn't sure if I had to fight him or what—I wasn't really looking forward to having any beefs with anybody.

The guy came back with my notebook after about an hour and said, "I want you to teach this at our Bible study."

"Who me?" I backpedaled. "I ain't really no preacher

or nothing."

"Bible study is in my cell." He completely dismissed my attempt to weasel out of prison preaching. "It'll be a few of us in there."

One of the guys I would talk to from time to time walked by, so I stopped him and asked, "Who is that dude? He took my stuff and then told me to teach a Bible lesson!"

"Oh, that's Deacon D. You must've wrote down a sermon or something. He used to be a deacon at a church. He cool."

**A Preacher and a Prisoner**

Since the other guys I talked to could vouch for the rude deacon, I made my way down to the cell where I saw some guys standing. I went in and introduced myself, and with the approval of the deacon, I started my lesson. When I was done it was dead silent. I didn't know if what I was saying was good or bad, or if it made sense at all.

One of the guys broke the silence and said, "Not to change the subject or nothin' but you not supposed to be here. You a church boy."

"I know," I sighed. "My uncle is a pastor, and I've been in church all my life." I began to tell them where my church was and details about our ministry—they knew who my uncle was! They knew where his church was! It was awkward that they were familiar with my uncle because of his ministry, and here I was known in here for a crime.

"Yea, you definitely not supposed to be in here," one guy confirmed. "What you do?"

I was hesitant to tell them, and they could sense my uneasiness.

"Look man, we not gon' do nothin'. If you want help, you gotta tell us what the problem is."

I had been so bent on keeping to myself and focusing on getting out, that I was always leery of sharing too much. These guys seemed like that truly wanted to help, so I told them all the details.

"But why would you date somebody that young?" The questions started to roll in.

"Man, I was really naïve and really didn't have much knowledge of those type of laws."

"Don't get me wrong," another dude interjected, "but that was nothing but an attack of the enemy. You had a huge calling on your life and so he set you up. He always tempts us with the desires of our hearts, and that's how he got you. That's what turns you prideful because you think you have everything and you don't need anybody."

He was 100 percent right. Elena was beautiful, supportive, caring, encouraging—everything that I had desired in a woman—but being involved with her cost me too much. I turned my back on God and everybody else. I feel like she was a pawn in this great quest to take me down!

They became more interested in my story.

"When you came in, where did they take you?"

I told them all of the places I had been, and how they kept moving me higher and higher in the jail.

This is the last stop," one solemnly declared. "How many times you been to the judge?"

"Man, I don't even know."

Then the Deacon interjected. "That's why the judge keeps denying you. God is trying to teach you something and bring you back to him."

I couldn't even say anything.

"God was breaking you down. He knew that if you would have turned around and went right back home, you wouldn't have changed. He wouldn't have been able to reach you. You are not supposed to fit in with everybody, and that's why you stand out here. You really have a purpose and a calling on your life. Don't be depressed about this, look at this as a wake-up call."

Some of these guys actually visited the church that my uncle built, and here they were speaking life into me.

**A Renewing**

When my next family visitation came, I couldn't wait to tell my mom that there were people in here who had been to the church!

"Ma, they came to the grand opening of the church, and they know unc!"

She was amazed. I told her all about how I was teaching sermons and getting encouragement while I was in here. My mom was a little uncomfortable with me being so excited about those guys, so like any mother would, she told me to watch my back just in case.

"Ma, I don't think these guys tryna do anything to me. They know that I have a calling and they're trying to help me stay focused so that I can get out of here."

"You've been stressed out." She studied the gray hairs that had peaked out on my face and the ungroomed hair on my head. I hadn't had a haircut or anything sense I'd been taken from my mother's house, and I knew that I needed a new image. I was no longer in a state of despair and depression. I had received a glimmer of hope and faith, and I wanted all of that to reflect on the outside.

When I went back to my cell, I walked past a couple of younger guys who had some sweet haircuts. Their cuts didn't look like the standard bald haircuts that some guys would get from the "official" barber. I immediately asked them who hooked them up, and out of all the guys, it was the deacon. Of course, I had to see him so that I could stop looking like a caveman. He told me that he was the one who did the lineups and that there was another guy who actually did the cuts with some makeshift clippers that he made from a broken razer and a rattail comb.

It was amazing to see how he was able to do a professional cut with just a few miscellaneous items from commissary. He gave me a salon experience: he shampooed my hair, conditioned it, and took time to make sure that my hair was just right. It kind of reminded me of what God was doing on the inside of me. He was using this time to groom me spiritually after I had searched for him to do just that. He needed to cut away the things that made me displeasing in his sight. My soul needed a makeover, and like the barber, God used the most unlikely combination of things to get the job done. I went to see the deacon, too, and felt a little like myself again.

I went back to the judge again, and he told me that I

didn't look like I belonged there. This time, I didn't ask for a personal bond—I figured if God was still trying to develop some things in me and remove some others, I wouldn't be released until he allowed it anyway. I did tell the judge that I had definitely learned my lesson, and that basically I was at his mercy. I wasn't sure if this would be convincing, but I wasn't going to crumple if I couldn't go home.

Sometimes satan will use negativity and challenges to hold over our heads and haunt or discourage us, but when we pray, motivate ourselves, and put our focus back on God, we can conquer what the enemy set up to destroy us. As I continued to seek God, and study his word, and as he continued to humble me, renew my mind and surrounded me with people who were encouraging me, I had favor. God began to use me to reach other young men who felt captive in their minds and were looking for someone to inspire them. I begin teaching bible classes, lead prayers, give advice—and it was right there that God revealed to me my purpose and my destiny.

My mother told me that my entire family went to church one Sunday and devoted that service to praying for me. Aunties, cousins, and everything. I was so moved that they were interceding on my behalf! While they were praying for me, I was in jail teaching a sermon called "The Spiritual

Love vs. the Fleshly Love". I had gone from teaching a room of about ten guys to teaching the entire floor—almost 125 men were receiving biblical teaching from me. I didn't expect that men of all ages would be listening.

I met one guy who had been in for past due tickets, and he came up to me and said, "Man, you look like you're not trying to get comfortable in here."

"If I settle and get comfortable then I'll never go home."

For someone who was there for some tickets, he had plenty of solid advice to give: "When you go before the judge again, make sure you have on a fresh new uniform. You already have a haircut so you'll look well-groomed. Ask them for a personal bond."

I was annoyed. I had asked for a personal bond plenty of times before and I ended up coming right back to my cell each time.

After a while, my previous cellmate had moved out and got his own cell, so I was alone. I saw D as a big brother figure, so I decided to room with him until I was able to go home. We were discussing my case, and D had said the same thing that I had been hearing over and over again: "Ask for a personal bond." At this point I was thinking that if "personal bond" was a person, I'd have slapped him by now. But D reassured me that I would get it the very next time I went to court. "Look the judge in the eye. Tell him that you were wrong and that you aren't a danger to society. Tell him that you have learned your lesson."

**Judgment Day**

As days passed by, I heard my name called to return back to court, I prepared myself physically and mentally. As I arrived to court, my mind was at peace and I had now put everything in God's hands. I made sure that I had followed all of the advice that I received for the other guys: fresh uniform, fresh socks, fresh shoes, new haircut. When I arrived, I was chained and put into a holding cell with about ten other men. We were packed into the room, and I couldn't help but think about how slaves were chained and packed into ships.

Before I came out, my attorney rushed in to speak to me. He told me that I couldn't come out yet because Elena was there. I didn't know whether to be upset, relieved, afraid, or what. I didn't know what reason she would have for showing up. The prosecutors didn't think it was a good idea for her to be present, so I had to wait for her to leave before the judge could try my case.

Standing before the judge, I couldn't help but feel like I was standing before God. He was seated high up behind the bench in a robe with a gavel that seemed to be ten times its normal size. The prosecutor, who was a woman, was pacing the floor; I figured that she would try her best to get the book thrown at me if she had personally thought that I had taken advantage of Elena. She had this mean look on her face, and I knew that this was it for me. I remember the judge looking at me saying I looked like I didn't belong or deserve to be locked up, but I was thinking *because of this, I was led back and reconnected to my heavenly father.*

The prosecutor presented her case: "Your honor, I think that he should have a little more time to make sure that he has learned his lesson."

My lawyer was clutch: "He already did 30 days, how much more time does he need?"

The judge asked both of them to approach the bench, but then he started to direct his attention to me.

"How was it in there?" It was an odd question, but I made sure that I answered clearly and truthfully.

"Honestly, I'm not used to this. I've never been in trouble before and I don't recommend that anybody be here.

But if anything, being here affirmed my purpose and calling in life."

"So, you learned your lesson?"

"Yes, I did!" I nearly interrupted. "I made a mistake, but I also learned that one mistake shouldn't define a person because life is about making mistakes, learning, and growing. My life isn't perfect, and I'm going to make more mistakes, but I've learned that there are consequences for my mistakes. I should be more careful with the mistakes that I make. I'm not a threat to anybody. I'm 19 years old, and I have more maturing to do."

He just stared at me. "You really don't look like you belong here. You have the face of a child—of a baby."

"Your honor, you can ask anyone who knows me. I'm not a bad guy, and I'm probably one of the nicest guys that you could ever meet. I'd rather help people out than be stuck in here."

The judge started talking and I whispered to my attorney, "Please ask him if I could have a personal bond." My attorney did as I wished and asked the judge for the bond. The prosecutor changed her entire attitude. At first she looked upset and offended by me, but she told the judge that she didn't see anything wrong with the personal bond. It had to have been the Holy Ghost.

The personal bond was granted. I had to sign off on some paperwork, but I really didn't know what all of it meant, so I asked my attorney.

"They're going to let you go home."

I froze. Tears began to well up in my eyes. I feared that if I blinked, rivers would start to flow on my face. I sat in my holding cell trembling and holding the yellow freedom papers that I had finally obtained. The guys around me in the holding cell asked what my papers said, and I let them read it.

"Man, soon as we get back, you out! Can I have your commissary and your snacks?"

We went back to the cell and told D that I was going home. He smiled and asked for my snacks, too. When everybody found out I was leaving, I felt like Oprah: *You get a snack, you get a snack, everybody gets a snack!* I gave away everything I had, and D said that he would make sure that the rest of my commissary items were distributed evenly.

I sat for about a good thirty minutes, reflecting on all of the days I spent there. I thanked God for allowing me to come out of this with my sanity intact.

D sat beside me and had even more words for me:

"When you get out of here, don't you come back!"

"Oh man I promise you that! If you ever see me again, it won't be in here!"

"If you come back, I'm fighting you. Forreal."

I chuckled and thanked him for all he had done for me. I probably would have been a wreck had it not been for him snatching my notebook that day. They called my name, and I began to walk towards my freedom. It felt so good putting on my normal clothes again.

In life, there are no perfect roads, there will be bumps, and curves and dangerous highways to cross. As long as God is the driving force, everything will be alright. The judge put me on probation and I was able to return home. Listening to the stories my family told me brought joy to my heart, and my mind was at peace because I realized that I made it through one battle and I conquered the obstacles.

# CHAPTER 4

## *The Actions of Thinking*

JUST BECAUSE WE MAY HAVE WON THE FIRST battle, and everything seems to be going well, it doesn't mean that another attack won't be coming our way. Satan will attack our minds before he attacks anything else. The Bible says, "When I want to do good, evil is always present (Romans 7:21)." Satan will always be present no matter what, but only this time, he'll come from a different direction and the battle is much greater. So what actions do we take when the obstacle or battle is something that we least suspect?

Sometimes if we are not careful with the way we think, our thoughts will begin to influence our feelings. If there is no resolution to whatever our thoughts may be, our feelings will influence our actions, and we won't realize that we have choices. How do our feelings play a role? Our feelings are only controlled through our thinking: when a person thinks happy or positive thoughts, his or her actions will be more positive. If a person thinks hurtful thoughts, his or her actions will reflect that hurt and anger. I call it an emotional cycle: the mind houses the thinking, the thinking regulates the feelings, and the feelings perform in actions. Take a second to allow your mind to think about a situation you've experienced. How do you feel about it? What actions did you take?

In my personal life, I went through different situations that had me taking action based on my feelings. Sometimes my actions were good, but then there were those times when my feelings had consumed me, and my actions caused me to experience some dangerous situations. I've already talked about being at the bottom, dealing with inner mind battles, and being in jail. I was able to bounce back with prayer and the support of my family and friends, but moreover, I was able to come out of that situation because I changed my thinking. I went from feeling like a victim and allowing my pride to overcome, to feeling more humble about what I was going through so that my actions could help me get back into relationship with God.

The enemy will stop at nothing to destroy us. His goal is to steal, kill and destroy. He is an opportunist; he only moves or takes action when he sees an opportunity. So what do you do when you're facing obstacles, battles and situations when you least expect them? What would be your thoughts when your guards are let down for just a second just because you thought you had overcome a particular situation and then the enemy strikes? What feelings would you have? How would you handle it?

**Home**

When I got back home, I literally kissed the ground. It felt so good to be free! I went in and saw my sister and my niece. My niece wasn't walking yet before I went to jail, and there she was now toddling all around the house. My mom and sister were telling me about how my younger brother had been getting into trouble and talking back—I couldn't wait to see him. He needed to know about my experience. He needed to know that jail wasn't a place he wanted to be. When he came home, I made him promise me that he would never end up there. He must have felt some type of shame because he promised me without any type of argument or stipulations.

When I came home, I was a lot smaller than I was before. My mother took me to a Coney Island and I probably ordered one whole side of the menu. I refused to eat the jail's version of food. The trays were disgusting and I just couldn't bring myself to do it. I survived on junk: cupcakes, chips, honeybuns—anything but their food. They gave us something that everyone referred to as "tea" to drink, which I later learned was just roof water. *Roof water.* The guys called it tea because it had a tint to it—like tea. There were people drinking it like it was nothing, and I figured that those guys had probably been in there too long.

**The Accuser of the Brethren**

I was getting used to being back at home, and I started to feel like myself again. I guess satan wasn't satisfied with the peace I had been experiencing because it was brought to my attention that one of my brothers was telling people that I was dead. *Yes, dead.* Like in the grave, on the front of a t-shirt, pictures of people with photoshopped angel wings dead.

He posted pictures on his Facebook page saying, "Rest in Peace" and everything. I was confused and hurt at the same time. To be honest, I didn't even know why he did it, but I always felt that there was a competition between us. Growing up, my relationship with my brother was tight—well I thought it was. It was like he wanted to be the oldest one or tried to be better than me—so I guess the opportunity came and he used it to his advantage.

In my family, we have a certain adage: everyone doesn't need to know family business. Period. We all must stick together and have each other's backs. After the whole "Wayne is dead" thing died down—obviously because people saw me walking around *living*—I found out that my brother told the whole world about my situation. People on our block, in the church, and my other family members all knew the reason for me being in jail. Granted, I take full responsibility for the decisions I made, but as a brother, he didn't cover me. He literally turned into "the accuser of the brethren". My brother was calling me stupid, and making fun of the situation. I could have responded in a negative way but I didn't, I could have taken action but I couldn't. I didn't want my negative thoughts to produce negative feelings. Moreover, I didn't want my ill feelings towards my brother to result in me doing something that I would later regret. I began to realize that sometimes God will expose you to save you, but it was hard to attend church services because I was thinking about the reaction of the people: *would they embrace me or throw stones?*

Sometime in church, you will have an encounter with both sides of the fence: some people will embrace you with love and encouragement and others are just there just waiting for you to fail. In my case, I pressed despite what anyone thought of me. I knew that I could never stop them from saying what or how they felt, so I let it roll off of me. The first time I walked in the church after my release, I noticed the joy that people had when they saw my face and it brought tears to my eyes. It felt good being around people who loved, supported, and prayed for me—my brother was bothered by all of the love and support I was receiving! I was still full of joy and I wanted to bury the hatchet between us. I knew at the end of the day, he would always be my little brother and it was my job to protect and show him forgiveness. We reconciled that Sunday.

**Temptation**

When I got home, I decided to set up a Myspace

account so that I could keep in touch with the people I had lost contact with before I went to jail. I didn't really have much activity going on, but one day I did receive a message. It was from Elena. She was telling me about how she was sorry and how she missed me so much—she wanted to see me so that we could talk about what happened. I wasn't going to do it. I couldn't afford to go backward. Days went by and she kept messaging me; I ignored her messages and continued to adjust to life back at home without her.

One day, my brother and I decided to go to our neighborhood park to play basketball. It was great getting back to some of my old activities and hanging out with my old friends. I turned around after making a shot, and Elena was standing right on the sidelines of the court. It was like some scary movie type of stuff. It was the first time that I had seen her since I'd been out, but I didn't stand around to talk to her or anything, I just left. The first thing that came to my mind was "run". I knew it upset her, but she cost me too much, and I didn't have any more time—or freedom—to give to her.

That was one day that I was successful at avoiding Elena, but it didn't stop the attacks of Satan. She kept messaging me and sending people to talk to me on her behalf;

the girl was relentless. I started to remember all of the good times and the special moments that we shared. My guard was down; I thought the strength I had before was enough, but I didn't realize that satan had turned things up just a little bit.

Eventually, I began to respond to her. All of the emotions that I stuffed down on the inside began to surface, and I found myself just wanting to know why she had betrayed me. She said that she was afraid and that she panicked. When you're in the presence of temptation and you find yourself trying to dig up the past, you give the enemy a chance to move. I felt a rekindling between us, even though I thought that the soul-tie that I had with her before was broken.

My mom, being the type of mom that she is, decided to check my phone one day, and she noticed that I had been communicating with Elena. She turned my phone off, and warned me again of the consequences of dealing with her. She even suggested that I live with my pops so that I didn't have to be around Elena, but I didn't really want to. Honestly, I got a little upset because I felt like that she didn't trust me, so I begin to plead with her, insisting that I didn't need to go there. I knew that I wouldn't have much freedom to do what I needed to do if I lived with my pops, so I promised my mom that I wouldn't talk to Elena anymore.

In the midst of trying to avoid Elena, my probation started. I reported to my officer and got a tether put on my leg. I thought that it would be nothing, but I didn't realize how much of a nuisance the tether was. I was on a strict schedule, and I could hardly do the things that I wanted to do when I wanted to do them. I couldn't just go outside and kick it with some friends: I either had to be going to work, looking for a job, or going to see my probation officer.

There would be times when my family was out taking care of business or doing whatever it was that they did during the day, and I was just alone in the house. I would look for things to watch on T.V., but eventually, that became mundane. There's a saying that an idle mind is the devil's playground, and that couldn't have been truer for me. The devil was having fun! I started to feel guilty about the situation I was in, and I really started to condemn myself. I felt like I was outside in a cage surrounded by the joy and the excitement of life, but I didn't have the key to set myself free. My family was going out enjoying life and there I was left alone.

One of the most dangerous times that our thoughts will speak the loudest is when we are by ourselves. When the enemy is settled into our minds, he'll begin to birth unusual thoughts such as discouragement, depression, defeat or even suicide I had spent time teaching and preaching to the men in the jail, but all that had gone out the window once I came home and faced reality. I started to feel like a failure—like I was a disappointment to everyone who was around me. I would spend my days with the blinds closed while sinking lower and lower into depression—again.

## A Battle with Death

I was at such a low point. I began to hear that familiar voice that I had heard taunting me while I was in jail: *You've already been to jail, and this is just like jail again. Do what anybody else in this situation would do—kill yourself.* The words were so convincing and the solution seemed so fitting. The more I thought, the more I dwelled on the possibility of ending my life. I went upstairs to my room, closed the door, and reached for a knife that I had hidden in my drawer. I had the knife positioned at my wrist and was all set to cut myself, when I heard another voice say, *Don't do it. Put your helmet back on and focus.* The voice was so clear. I looked around because nobody was there but me. I didn't have a phone anymore, so I knew that it couldn't have been that. I shook off my hesitation—this time I pointed the knife right at my chest. I told myself that I was going to count down and then stab myself in the heart. I began: one...two...and then I heard a voice interrupting me again. *Put your helmet back on. Focus on me, and hear me.*

I was sick with conviction. I put the knife down and sobbed. I went to the bathroom to dry my face and this voice that was clearly God said, *I haven't forgotten about you. I need you to get yourself together.* I could do nothing but fall on my knees and ask God for help.

*Lord, you got me out of this, but I don't feel free. I may be physically free, but I'm not mentally free.* I started to ask God to help me overcome the feelings of depression and suicide that seemed to taunt me time and time again.

I didn't speak a word of this to my mother or anybody else in my family. I didn't want them to worry. Even though I had heard God speak to me and tell me to put my helmet back on (meaning get back in the fight and rely on the God of my salvation), the enemy was still trying to conquer my thoughts. Since my mother had taken my phone, I asked her if I could use hers from time to time. You wouldn't believe it, but I found myself texting Elena. I knew that I should have nothing else to do with her, but I had convinced myself that I just needed to bring "closure" to what happened between us. One conversation turned into two, and the next thing I knew, we had made it a habit of conversing with each other and making plans to see each other.

### Moving Backwards

One day I told my mom that I was going to walk to Walmart—it was like 10 or 15 minutes away, so she said ok. While I was walking, I remembered that Elena called me earlier that day asking me to come by her house. We lived in a townhome complex, and her apartment was not far. Instead of me going to Walmart, I ended up making a detour to Elena. I told her to let me in the side door because I didn't want to get caught by my sister, who lived across from Elena's family. She told me that I couldn't come through the side door and suggested that I just run through the front door. *That made no sense at all.* Instead of me saying no, I ran through her front door just like she told me to.

I thought that I wouldn't get caught and that I was good. We sat inside her house and talked for a minute. I felt myself being in drawn back in with each second I was in her presence. As I was preparing to leave, I told her that I didn't want to go back out the front—I mean, I tried to open the side door and everything, but nothing worked. Trying my best not to get caught, I ran back out the front door and tried to make it seem like I took another way to get to Walmart. I went and bought a few things to secure my alibi, but as I was walking back home, I got a text from my mom saying that I was caught and that she had my sister watching me. I couldn't say anything. Not a word.

When I got back to the house, I saw all of my things packed up; I looked outside and saw my father pulling up. My mom called my probation officer and told him that I would be moving into a different residence. She explained to him that her house wasn't the best place for me to be because Elena lived in the neighborhood and had already made attempts to contact me. My P.O. agreed that I should leave; I remember thinking that it was the right move and then on top of that my probation was scheduled to start the next day. Somehow, living with my dad had to be the best plan for me—or so I thought.

# CHAPTER 5

## *"Pops"*

So, I moved in with my pops. The first conversation that we had was about my tether and my schedule. I told him that there would be times when I would need to be in the house, per the instructions of my P.O. Sometimes my pops has a habit of being a know-it-all, and he insisted that I come with him and his wife to Bible class that evening.

"Pops," I protested, "I shouldn't be out tonight because they'll know, and I don't want to get into any more trouble."

"They know you just moved and your equipment ain't even plugged in yet. You'll be alright."

***

My father and I have not always had the best relationship. Today, I could text or call him and have a full-blown conversation, but we had to overcome some major milestones to be where we are today. As a teenager, I felt like I could never talk to my father. He put the fear of God in us—living with him was sort of like walking on eggshells because I felt he was so far removed for us emotionally. I believe that being unable to express myself to my father or learn how to communicate with him in a healthy manner caused me to carry those terrible habits into my adulthood.

My probation period required me to have regular sessions with a therapist. I remember attending my first therapy session—I was sitting there listening to this stranger ask me all of these questions about my feelings, and thoughts. He wanted to know about specific situations that happened in my life, but I just sat there and said nothing. It was like I was afraid and didn't know how to open my mouth, but my thoughts were screaming and shouting in my head. Time and time again, I went back and forth to therapy without saying anything, but I kept bouncing around thoughts of everything that I'd been through and how I had lost everything. I kept battling those depressive and angry thoughts.

I remember sitting in front my probation officer, and he was explaining to me that the only way that I could progress in my probation process was to open up and talk. As he was sitting there expressing to me the importance of opening up, I was thinking about everything that I ever been through—from my parents being divorced, to what was taking place now, and how it all played a factor in my decision to almost commit suicide for the first time. I reflected on my deep depression, confusion, and stress. I mean, I was jobless and staying in a small room at my father's house. My life was literally at a halt. I begin to wonder if I would ever be free.

Before I left out the office, I looked at my probation officer and said, "Ok I'll give it a shot." I showed up for therapy, and sat on the couch. My therapist looked at me and asked if I was ready to talk—at that very moment, tears begin to roll down my face. I asked him if you can you truly let go of what you thought you let go of: the hurt, the pain, the anger, the guilt. *How do you let it go*? He told me that the only way to let go was to cut myself from the root of the challenges that I faced. He told me that opening up was the first step.

## Inside the Mind of a Conqueror

Understand that there will be times when you can be strong and still be in pain.

I honestly think that the root to all of this started when my father and mother got a divorce. My father left the house when I was 17 or 18 years of age. I felt like the pressure of being the man of the house was then placed on me since he was gone. I remember pleading with my father, asking him to come to an agreement with my mother and work things out for the sake of my brothers and sisters, but I saw the look he had in his eyes. I saw the pain and the hurt. There's this saying: "Hurt people will hurt people". My father looked at me and said, "I just wanna move on, and leave, and live my life." I felt like he didn't really fight for us.

I didn't know how to take it. Back then it seemed like he was saying "screw everybody" and it was all about him. At that time, I felt abandoned because I felt like his protection and guidance was no longer there. I remember asking him who I was supposed to look at to show me how to be a man. He was my example. I told him that if he left us, his covering would be gone. I felt like he tossed us to the wolves. And the wolves did come. My family was torn to shreds when he left.

Even after the divorce, I felt like he was still taking his anger with my mother out on us. He came to my graduation, and I remember enthusiastically telling him to watch me receive my diploma. As I stood in line, I turned around, and he was gone. I was confused and lost—so lost that I began to blame my mother because I felt like she didn't hurt as much as my brothers, sisters, and I did.

I poured out all of my pent-up feelings, and just like that, my therapy session was over. At the end of my session, my therapist asked a question, but I couldn't answer it right away because I had to really evaluate myself. He asked, "Why did you allow yourself to be tied and connected with situations that could be a threat to your potential?" I couldn't respond because at that time I really didn't understand the question. I begin to realize that I really struggled with that—holding on to unresolved situations and past hurts. I was dealing with past frustration that clashed with my present frustration. It was the catalyst for disaster.

"You have to learn how to forgive and let go of all of that. When you forgive people, it sets you free. You're free from the stronghold that unforgiveness has over you."

*\*\*\**

I went to church with my dad—as he insisted—and I was so embarrassed that I had this big black tether on my ankle. I had on shorts, so it was out and exposed for everyone to see. People kept coming up to me asking what exactly happened and how long I had to wear it. I got tired of all of the questions and attention. Then you have those few who want to tell you what you already know: "Well, let this be a lesson learned!" I didn't need to keep hearing that.

    I didn't have a job anymore once I came back home, so my goal was to try to find some type of employment as fast as I could. I would walk up and down major streets in my area and fill out job applications. This would be a daily routine for me, but the difficulty was that if I didn't leave the house when my pops or his wife left, I would be locked in. If I left when they did, I couldn't get back inside the house until they came home. This presented a major problem for me. If I was locked in, that meant that I literally couldn't get out. Whatever kind of lock that they had installed required that you have a key to get in and out of the house. Why I wasn't given a key was completely beyond me. If a fire broke out or I needed some type of emergency care, I would be sorely out of luck!

    The other part of the issue was that when I would be out looking for jobs, I still had a certain time to be back in the house to check in with my P.O. There were plenty of days that I had missed those check-in phone calls because I was locked outside of the house. Sometimes my mom would take me to the mall to fill out applications, and when she took me back to my pops's house, she saw that I couldn't get in. This caused my mom, dad, and stepmom, to argue plenty of times because my mom knew how important it was for me to not have any more strikes against me. I would tell my P.O. the situation and he didn't seem to have much sympathy for me.

**Forsaken**

This reoccurring inconvenience got so bad, that my mom found herself calling my stepmother and telling her how they needed to be home so that I wouldn't be getting in more trouble with my P.O. As an adult man, you feel kind of weird when your mom tries to "fight" your battles for you, but I appreciated her for having my back. I don't know everything that she said to my stepmom, but the next thing I knew, my stepmom was trying to confront me about the conversation that she had with my mother. She was very aggressive, and she was speaking to me just inches from my face.

*I hope she's not tryna boss up and fight me. Wayne, you're a man who doesn't hit women. You can't get into any fights, especially with her, or you'll be back in jail.*

I was trying to calm myself down and deescalate the situation, but I felt my blood boiling and my heart racing. My face must have been beet red because I was that furious. She wasn't helping me. Since I'd been here, neither of them acted like they cared about the things I needed to do. I knew that I couldn't hit her with my hands, so I decided to hit her with my words instead.

"You've never done anything for me. You'll always be second to my mom. You're not even a real mother at all because you never carried anybody for nine months. You'll never be a mother."

She froze. She backed up, went into her room and closed the door. I went in my room, too, and tried to process the entire ordeal. Of course, the situation got back to my pops, so then he and I started to argue.

"Even though she's not your mom, she still took you in!"

"If you're male or female, it doesn't give you the right to get in my face. She's walking up to me like she's a dude, and that's not cool at all."

"Just go apologize."

"No, I'm not. I'm not apologizing because both of y'all are messing me up! Every time I go to my probation officer, I'm getting in trouble, and y'all act like y'all don't care!"

He didn't say anything else, he just walked away. I went back in my room and gave myself a pep-talk: *You gotta go back to how you were. It's all about you—you gotta take care of yourself.* My mom kept calling, essentially accusing them of being bad parents and telling them that they needed to help me. She was right about the fact that they weren't really working with me, but I think how she went about it was wrong. There was still bad blood between my mother, father, and now stepmother regarding everything that had taken place before and after the divorce. I have a feeling that some of her frustration was still linked to some unresolved issues.

One day, she was about to drop me off, and they weren't there—again. I was just going to sit on the porch and wait, but this time, she wanted to wait, too. When they pulled up, my mom got out the car and just started going off! In the midst of my mom yelling, I simply asked my step-mother if she could open up the door so that I could be inside before my P.O. called. She took her time getting the keys and making her way to the door. I heard the phone ring, and I knew it was my P.O. I finally got inside to answer the phone. My P.O. asked me why I had been late answering his call, and I told him what I had already been telling him every time he asked. He just hung the phone up in my face. I was furious so I just went in the room and shut my door. My mom was still out there going back and forth arguing with my pops. Eventually, my pops came back inside and forcefully swung open my door.

"Look. I'mma tell you like this. I don't care about your situation, and I don't care about you."

Forget that knife that I had put to my own chest, my father stabbed me right through the chest with those words. How could he fix his mouth to say that me? To his *son*. I get that he was angry, but I feel like those words were coming from a different place.

"If I was up to me, I'd take this equipment and throw it out the window."

Immediately, all of those feelings that I had as a 17-year-old boy started bubbling to the surface. The thoughts of being uncovered and abandoned resonated in my mind. I remembered those times when I looked for my father to be my advocate and protector, and realizing that he was willing to walk away from that position because he just "wanted to live his life". I didn't realize how far removed we were from each other—strangers in the street had more love for each other than we had during this time.

I knew that if he threw my equipment out, it would mean serious trouble for me. My P.O would probably think that I was trying to escape or something. There would be no doubt that I would be back in jail. *This dude really don't care,*

I thought to myself. *I have to get out of here.*

As soon as I was able, I went to my P.O and explained to him, again, what was going on. I told him that it was best if I moved with my mom again, even though she was living with my sister.

"That's near a school. You agreed not to be in any school areas."

"I'm not a threat to anybody," I pleaded. "I'm just trying to do this the right way so that I can be done with all of this and move on with my life."

My P.O approved my request to live with my mom, so I went to my dad's, packed up my equipment, and told him that I was out. It felt good to leave.

# CHAPTER 6

## *Homeless and Hopeless*

WHEN I GOT TO MY MOM'S HOUSE AND SETTLED in, I remembered the weather being nice and everybody being outside, but it was on a day when I couldn't leave because of my probation. I was sitting in my bedroom, feeling discouraged and depressed, reflecting on what I'd done to put myself in this situation. I was thinking about how I had been going back and forth from one place to another and thinking about what happened at my pops's house. I needed to know how to get over the pain and the rejection that I felt. I felt like a failure and I couldn't escape my life. I felt abandoned.

Once I moved back with my mom, my first priority was to find a job. I had so many fees to pay—not to mention I was broke as ever—so I needed a way to get some money in my pockets. I ended up getting a job at one place, but I didn't want to tell my manager that I could only work morning shifts because I was on a tether. I remedied the situation by telling my probation officer that I needed more flexibility with my schedule, and he was fine with it as long as I was working.

So, I worked a few weeks, and things seemed to be on the up and up. That is until I looked out my mom's window one day and saw Elena walking slowly past our place. Even though my mom was able to get a new place, it was still in the neighborhood, and it meant that I would probably be seeing Elena again. I really felt like I couldn't shake this girl! I found myself finding excuses to walk by her house, and the next time I blinked, I was back inside sitting on her couch. I kept telling myself that I needed "closure" and that was the reason for the frequent visits and constant communication. It was so easy for other people to tell me to stay away from her, but no one knew the type of connection that we had. It was the very definition of a soul-tie—I was linked to her so deeply that she had influence over my mind, my will, and emotions. I felt like she had been woven tightly into each fiber of my being, and walking away from her was like walking away from myself.

I worked every day; if I didn't have a ride there, sometimes I would walk to and from work. It was so exhausting because some of those times I would walk home and miss curfew, so I would have to hear it from my P.O. God knows I didn't want to go through that situation again. One time, it was pouring raining when I had gotten off of work, and I had to walk about ten miles in the storm. I didn't get home until about two in the morning, and I had completely missed my curfew. I wanted to rest up and take the next day off, but I was on a mission. I still went to work the next day; I had to make this money to pay off theses fees!

**Man Down**

Then it so happened that as I was walking to work, I saw Elena—again. I tried to keep things very brief with her; she spoke and I spoke back. I didn't want to linger any longer with her because I knew that somehow, a little went a long way with her. If I had let my guard down just a little bit, should would have full access to me. I didn't need those types of problems—again.

After I had seen her that day, somehow she got my number—I'm guessing from one of my younger sisters—and sent me a link to a song. It was *our* song. Her message said, "Just listen to it." I caved and listened to the song. It immediately brought me back to some of the best times we had together. It reminded me of what it was like to have her in my life and for her to have my back when nobody else did. It made me think that there was some way that we could get that back. I was willing to risk whatever to have that "love" again.

We started back texting each other. The texting turned into conversations, and the conversations turned into her sneaking into my house late at night or early in the morning so that we could have sex. This situation continued for a while, and the soul-tie that was previously established was stronger than ever. I don't know why I didn't know better—it was almost like the fact that she was "forbidden" to me made we want to be with her that much more.

I was so caught up in her, that I started slipping. One time she was over, my mom came downstairs and saw someone leaving out of the patio door.

"Who was that?"

I am a terrible liar. I tried to make up something really

quick, but I couldn't. I just ended up telling her that it was Elena, and she had wanted to drop a letter off to me before she went to school. I tried to make her think that it was nothing to be alarmed about.

"I don't think that's a good idea, Jr." She had always been the one to warn me of the consequences of dealing with Elena, and like every other time, I didn't want to listen. I was thinking about how connected I was to Elena and how I didn't really know how to break free from that tie, but I had told my mother that there was nothing to worry about. Inside, I knew that I was falling into another ditch, and I was digging it deeper.

### Down and OUT

I should have seen it coming, because my mom had warned me before. She had found out that I was seeing Elena again, and just like the last time she found out about us, she put me out. I couldn't even blame her, it was really the only thing that she explicitly asked of me, and I knew that it was for my own good.

I called Elena and told her what had happened and how I didn't have anywhere to go. I couldn't go back with my dad because we were still angry with each other, so Elena told me that I could bring my things to her house. I went there and put all of my things in her closet, but I still didn't understand how this could work. I was ordered to stay away from her, but now I'm thinking about living with her? I suggested that I sleep on her floor, but it was too risky. Some nights I slept on the playscape behind her townhouse, other nights she let me sleep in her mother's car—there were some nights that I didn't sleep at all because the idea of having no roof over my head didn't really put me in a relaxing state of mind.

I was still going to work every day, but then I found out that I was being laid off because business had slowed down. Perfect timing, right? I was still on probation, but of course I didn't tell my P.O that I had gotten kicked out of my mother's house, loss my job, and was now technically homeless. My P.O said that he wanted to come by my house to do an inspection just to make sure that I was meeting all of the requirements of my probation, and I didn't know what to do. I called my little sister and told her to make it look like I still lived there so that my P.O wouldn't be suspicious. My mom told me that I wasn't welcome back in the house, so I was going to sit on the porch during his visit and play it cool. When he came, luckily my mom wasn't there, but after he left, I still had nowhere to go. I would take what little money I had and go to the movies or go and sit inside of a fast food restaurant. When Elena's pops wasn't home, I would spend a few hours there. I know. I was playing with fire.

I was thinking about begging my mother for forgiveness and coming back home, but she and my sisters had eventually moved out of state. When I talked to my mom, she told me to call my dad so that I could have somewhere to live, but I refused. There was no way that I could go back to that man's house again. Besides, he had told my mom that he'd take my younger brother in, but never me. He said that he was tired of dealing with me like I was such an inconvenience to his life.

My cousin came to pick my brother and me up, and he asked me where I was going to go if I wasn't going to my father's house. I just told him to drop me off on 16 Mile and Vandyke. I was walking up the street with no money and no place to go. I went back to Elena's house, but nobody was there, so I continued to walk aimlessly trying to figure out a plan. I slept under a few bridges, and somehow managed to spend some time in an old arcade. Elena's dad starting using her mom's car more often, so sleeping there wasn't a good option anymore. Eventually I became desperate. My aunt called me and suggested that I tell my pops that I would agree to pay some of the rent and utilities if he allowed me to stay with him, but even in my desperation, my pride dismissed that idea completely. *If my younger brother didn't have to make that deal with him then why should I have to?* Besides, he kept saying no anyway.

One of those nights when I was walking up and down the street, my pops called. He asked me where I was, and I told him that I was just walking up and down Vandyke trying to figure out what I was going to do. He told me to just come to his house. When I got there, he had this look on this face like he really didn't want me there.

"I'm doing this because you're my son, but we're going to have to talk more about this in the morning."

That night I slept on the floor, but I couldn't stomach the idea of being in my father's house unwanted. The next morning, I told my pops, "Look, I know you don't want me here, and I don't want to be anywhere I'm not wanted." I ended up taking what little things I had and ended up heading right back to Elena's house.

I ended up using Elena's computer to put in a million job applications, and one of those places called me within a few hours of submitting my application. They called me in for an interview, but I didn't really have many clothes, let alone "interview clothes". I had been in the clothes I had on during the time they called me for about three days, but I managed to put something together so that I could look presentable.

I ended up walking there and meeting with the manager. The interview went fairly well, and the manager asked me when I could start. I looked the man square in the face and told him that I could start right then, but he told me that they couldn't make an immediate decision and that they'd be in touch.

After I left the interview, I went back to Elena's house and freshened up a bit so that I could take the bus back to my pop's house. When I got there, nobody was home, and I didn't want to just sit on the porch and wait for them to get back, so I went walking—again—up the road until I found a Walmart to sit around in for a while. I had been there for some time, and I didn't want to seem suspicious, so I left and went somewhere else to eat. My mom called me a few times, and when I finally answered, I just wanted to break down.

"How have you been?"

"I feel like giving up, ma. You'd think that I'd had some family that would take me in, but I had nobody."

"Everything is going to be alright," she attempted to console me, but I had gotten tired of hearing that. I was a

## Inside the Mind of a Conqueror

grown man who was constantly being pacified with promises of better days, but *when* would those better days come?

# CHAPTER 7

## *Battle Stage of the Mind*

"*F*OR MY THOUGHTS ARE NOT YOUR THOUGHTS, *neither are your ways my ways, saith the Lord.*" (Isa.55:8)

Have you ever been in a situation where your thoughts were straddling the fence? Have you ever prayed and expected God to answer, but instead, you get silence? Sometimes we can experience challenges or obstacles that we just know God is going to fix, but instead, he responds with silence.

## Inside the Mind of a Conqueror

In life, we face obstacles and battles, and when we don't have a clue what to do, we can allow our thoughts to enter the "Should I, or should I not?" Syndrome. The word "syndrome" is defined as a group of symptoms that together are characteristic of a specific disorder, disease, or the like. It's a predictable characteristic pattern of behavior or action that tends to occur under certain circumstances. When we don't have guidance or someone to lead us, we allow are our thoughts to form the question *Should I or should I not?* This question can especially be present in the mind when making major decisions pertaining to relationships, goals, jobs, and other things prevalent in our lives.

*But* what do you do when you're in a war zone, and your leader, your captain—which is God—is silent? He's still present, but he won't mumble a word to help you out. He sees what's ahead of you, but his still small voice becomes still*er* and small*er*. Sure, he's answered the prayers you've prayed before—and he's brought you out of some foul mess before. But has it ever occurred to you that he's so silent because he's testing your faith?

How much patience do you really have? When it comes down to the last straw and you're placed back into darkness, will your praise and worship be the same as it was before? Truth be told, sometimes God will position us back in the same situation we thought we overcame just to see what our first reaction will be. The majority of us will question ourselves, and fall victim to "Should I or Should I Not?" Syndrome.

My mind generated these questions: *What did I do or say that made my father not want me there? Was it the situation with my stepmom? If so, she tried to confront me! Should I go back to my past to get help, or should I press forward and hope for the best?*

I was just rehearsing my circumstance over and over to myself: my mother has left with my baby brother and sister, my other brother was with my father, and I was out on the street. I remember continuously calling my mom asking why my father didn't want me there, and she kept saying that she didn't know. I had to learn that sometimes God will put you in a place where it seems like you're wandering in the wilderness—where your mama isn't able to help you and your father didn't want to deal with you—and your only option was to call on Jesus. I begin to pray and ask God for direction and guidance, but there was still silence.

Walking up and down the streets, tears in my eyes, I allowed my thoughts to straddle between my past and my future. I thought about drinking away my pain. It seemed to be the only solution to the depression I was facing. I used to hear people say, "If you want the tears to go away, drink 'til your pain fades away." I was hell bent on drowning away my sorrows for sure. I took the few dollars that I had and bought a bottle of 1800. I remember my family pleading with my father to take me in, but still nothing happened. The crazy part about all of this is that I have a big family, and no one offered me a place to stay. At this point, my mind and body was tired. I remember my mom calling me and asking me where I was and what I was doing. I could always hear the sound of worry in her voice, so I would tell her, "Mom I'm going to be alright, don't worry."

**Called into the Deep**

With tears in my eyes, I was sitting by a little lake, trying to drink the pain away. As I was sitting there, drunk and all, the sun had gone down, and a voice spoke to my mind saying, *I wonder how deep is this little lake is*. Staring at the lake, the voice continued talking saying, *Take a swim. You need to drown your sorrows*. I was tempted to drown my sorrows along with my lungs. I begin thinking and debating—should I or should I not?

It's crazy because if we are not careful in dealing with

our sorrows suicidal thoughts can easily seep into our mind, and the enemy will give reasons to take your own life. Whenever you're at your lowest point in life, whether you're depressed, confused, or feeling abandoned, satan can remind you of the negative things that happened in your life. He may begin to feed your mind ways to take your life, such as drinking or turning to drugs. He may even tempt you with the thought of killing someone because of anger. If we are not careful, it may seem real to us, but it will only be an illusion of what God has brought us from; satan just presents our past in a negative way. Sometimes God can be speaking but because we've allowed our minds to be cluttered with doubt, fear, and other thoughts that did not originate from God, it may seem like he is silent

**The Work of Patience**

After a while, I began to take matters into my own hands because I felt like I didn't have any guidance or direction. I couldn't figure out if God was responding or not. God's silence can also be a test of our faith, and sometimes we have to pray and ask God to humble us and give us the mind to be patient. Patience is the ability to withstand provocation or annoyance without complaint. Patience is also quiet, steady perseverance—the Bible says in Isaiah 40:31 *"They that wait upon the lord shall renew their strength; they shall mount up with wings as eagles; they shall run, and not be weary; and they shall walk, and not faint." (KJV).*

While I was going through my time of extreme misfortune, I didn't have patience. The little patience that I did have ran very thin, and I think it was because I was tired of going through and looking forward to something that was blurry in my vision and in my thinking. Even in the midst of my cloudy thinking, I started to talk to God like he was right there with me. Sometimes you have to talk to God like you're in a therapy session—put it all out on the table. He already knows what's in your heart and mind but it's something about just hearing it from our lips. It's like a parent responding to a child—the parent already knows that the child will hurt himself from time to time, but it's when the parent hears the sound of the child's cry that moves him and causes him to comfort the child.

I didn't want to wrap my thoughts around the fact that I was homeless, so there I was back wandering the streets day by day, trying to figure out what my next move would be. Whenever you find yourself in the "Should I, Should I Not?" stage, not only will your thoughts be pacing back and forth, but you'll also find yourself pacing from one area to another, with no desire to just be still. You can't hear and recognize God's voice or see the direction he wants you to go in while you're pacing. That's why God said in 2 Chronicles 20:17 *"Ye shall not need to fight in this battle, set yourself, stand ye still and see the salvation of the Lord with you."*

**Be Halted**

When we set our minds and our thoughts are still, we will see the move of God, even in dark situations. It may be dark but that doesn't mean that God is absent. Understand that God will defend, fight and move on our behalf because number one, we are his children and he love us, and number two, we have decided to be in a halted position while he's moving. The word halt means to stop; cease moving; to cause to stop temporarily or permanently. People always ask the question, "If God loves us why does he allow this to happen or that to happen?" The truth is that God does love us, but he hates the sin that we do. Whenever sin is committed, there are consequences, but in the midst of those consequences, God shows his love through mercy and grace.

God also shows his love in John 3:16, *"For God so love the world that he gave his only begotten son, that whosoever believe in him should not perish but have everlasting life."* If and when we plant that in our minds and come to a halted position, we will see God in action. I think the problem is that we can be impatient. I've learned that sometimes we wish that life itself was stress free and problem free, but I realize that if life was like that we wouldn't need God. I know that God will allow things to happen in our lives so there is an opportunity for him to show us that we need him. God uses some things we go through to destroy our prideful spirits and to humble us.

Whenever we face obstacles, God gives us words to encourage and strengthen us; it is satan who feeds our thoughts with negativity. I decided to place myself in a halted position. I remember walking to a Meijer store, going into the bathroom, and sitting in the last stall. I told myself that this was where I was laying my head that night, and wasn't going to move. There I was, in a messed-up situation, but I was in the right position. All of a sudden, I got a phone call from my father saying that he wanted to talk to me. We talked for nearly 40 minutes after not speaking to each other for weeks. He asked me where I was, and when I told him, he opened up his home to me again. In that moment, I realized that God had never left. There's a saying that I've heard my entire life: "God may not come when you want him, but God is always on time." He was definitely on time for me.

I realized that I never should have let doubt and fear

clutter my thinking. I should always set my focus on God's word. Matthew 6:33-34 says, *"Seek ye first the kingdom of God, and his righteousness; and all these things shall be added unto you. (34) Take therefore no thoughts for the morrow; for the morrow shall take thought for the things of itself."* How can we prevent ourselves from having the "Should I or Should I Not?" Syndrome? By seeking God first in all that we do and before we do anything. No matter what our situations may be, or the obstacles we may face—even if it may seem like God is silent—get into a halted position and hold on to his word.

Psalms 55:22 says, *"Cast thy burden upon the lord and he shall sustain thee: he shall never suffer the righteous to be moved."*

Romans 8:28 says, *"And we know that all things work together for good to them that love God, to them who are the called according to his purpose."*

These scriptures are what helped me realize that no matter what battles I faced or have had an encounter with, God is always there. So now that he answered and brought me out of the obstacles, what do you do when you are betrayed by those who say they love you and want the best for you?

# CHAPTER 8

## The Aftermath of Thinking

THE AFTERMATH OF THINKING IS OUR REACTION after going through or dealing with different situations that occur in our lives. Sometimes it can be good in the beginning and the end can be bad. How do we face new consequences? What new steps do we take? What type of thinking should we have? Is it fixable? Is there enough patience and motivation in us to fix it or deal with it? When thinking about the challenges that we face, do we really *face* them? Do we run from them, or do we stand and do nothing? We can answer these types of questions after we have been through obstacles, battles, and the challenging situations. Who do I turn to? A lot of times we face these things and the first thing our thoughts tell us to do is to confide in the people in our inner circle.

**Be careful who you let in your camp because there are those who can be in your circle causing you to lose the battles that you face.**

Sometimes the people that we have in our lives are not always there to encourage us, but they are there as news reporters. They want to know the information just to broadcast it to the public. Some people only want to be in your life to betray you and want you to see you fail. How would we handle that? There were times in my own personal life when I always found myself being distant from people or the crowd because of trust issues, and because I was afraid of being judged or looked at differently because of what they might've heard.

**Unsettled**

When I returned to my pops's house, I was still a little unsettled about being there. He woke me up early the next morning to talk, but honestly, it was going in one ear and out the other. I had so many thoughts swirling in my head, but I couldn't fix my mouth to say much. *I gotta bounce back. This sucks.*

If I wasn't on probation, I would have probably lived with my mom down south. She would have let me in. Moms have a way of whooping you and then loving you at the same time. I realized that I had betrayed her trust by seeing Elena behind her back, but she still wouldn't have me homeless.

My brother hadn't see me in a while so he was concerned.

"You good, Wayne?"

"No," I admitted. "It's hard waking up every day knowing that you really don't have a place to stay and no real income. On top of all of that, I have to keep going to these probation meetings. I feel like I'm not in control of my own life. I feel like I'm locked up still because I gotta answer to all these people."

At my next probation meeting, my P.O. and I had the same circular conversation we always have about me needing to find a job and getting back on my feet. I felt like he really didn't have to tell me that—*of course* I needed a job! *Of course,* I need to get back on my feet!

"If you're staying at your dad's house, that's where you

need to be because we're checking on you." I couldn't not wait to get off of probation. The constant monitoring was getting to me.

So, I got up and begun my search for employment. It was hard but, I never quit because I was walking by faith—the confidence or trust in a person or thing. My faith was in God because I knew my word: "Faith is the substance of things hoped for and the evidence of things that are not seen (Hebrews 11:1)." I understood that even though I was in a tough situation, God revealed to me that I can do not just some things but all things through him because it is him that strengthens me.

I ended going back to the job that I had before I went to jail, and I was surprised to be able to get my job back. This was such a huge relief. I felt like things had started to work in my favor a little bit. I had been trusting God through all of this, and now I felt like I was starting to see the fruit of all of my prayers and tears. I was a host, a busser, and dishwasher, and I made sure that I gave it my all. I became employee of the month and God was still blessing me.

Sometimes faith will cause you to feel like you've lost everything, but eventually you will gain so much more. There were times when not just my faith but the level of it had been

tested. When we are walking by faith, God will allow things to happen that we are unprepared for mentally and physically just to see if our faith will increase or decrease. I was so caught up
in the blessing of God that I didn't prepare myself for what was to come. I should have been preparing by praying and asking God to give me the mind, and strength to overcome those pending obstacles and challenges.

**Pops, Round Two**

What type of thinking are you supposed to have when the challenge or battles you face are within your own family? When it's with the people who say that they love you and support you? What do you do when you're being lied on, and instead of both stories being heard, your story gets ignored? How would you handle it or face it? What type of thoughts would be in your mind?

There was one time I came home from work and my pops asked me if I had seen some DVD movies. I was thinking, *Man, my pops think I'm stealing. I'm about to get put out again.* I told him that I hadn't seen them, and then—to my relief and my disappointment—he told me that he thought my brother had stolen them.

"Do you have any proof?" I really didn't want to get

between my pops and my brother, but I felt that he should have at least asked him about it.

"They were sitting right here."

The next thing I knew, my pops and my stepmother were arguing with my brother, and they eventually kicked him out. He ended up staying with his girlfriend, and I called him to find out what was going on.

"Wayne, I ain't did nothin'," he explained. "I don't have any movies, and I didn't steal anything."

"I know," I smacked my lips and shook my head, "You gotta understand that it ain't pops though, it's *her*. They feel like we're taking up their personal space. I'm next. I don't know when it's going to happen, but I know I'm next." I really felt like ever since my dad remarried, he changed a lot. I suspected that his new wife had a lot to do with it.

I tried to keep my distance while I was staying with my pops. I found myself always staying in my room or trying my best to be gone when they were home. There was no communication, or no bonding time. I felt like that they really didn't want me there. I remember my father telling me that I can talk to him about any and everything, but I just found that hard to believe. I just resolved to keep working so that I could get out of there soon.

## Get Out!

Then I became "next" just like I told my brother. There was one day that my stepmother and I were heading to Bible class, and we got into a bad argument. I told her that I wanted a key to be able to get in. I explained to her that I was working and paying them every week—it was reasonable for me to have a key so that I could come and go as I pleased. She didn't like that idea. I didn't understand why she was set against me having access to their home unless she didn't want me there at all. That conversation escalated quickly, and it didn't end on a good note.

While we were on the way to Bible class, she brought up what we were talking about earlier that day, and I just didn't want to go there again with her. I just wanted to go to Bible class, get me a good word in, and go about my day. She obviously wasn't settled so she started yelling and cursing.

"I'm not about to sit up here and let you holler and cuss at me!" I shouted.

We were driving up the freeway, and she pulled the car over and screamed, "Get out!"

I got out and slammed the door, and my stepmother drove off. Tears begin to roll down my face because I didn't look at her as just a stepmom but an evangelist in the church.

## Inside the Mind of a Conqueror

I called my mom and told her what happened, so she immediately called my pops. I already knew what was about to happen. I was about to be on the street *again*.

So, there I was, walking up and down the street again, trying to figure out what was about to happen. My pops called my phone saying the most ridiculous thing I'd ever heard come out of his mouth.

"She told me that you cussed at her *and* you put your hands on her!"

"Man, *what?*" I yelled. I completely lost it at that point. This is the second time that this woman had falsely accused me or something. I just broke down in tears. "Pops, if anybody knows me, *you* do. You know that I don't hit women! I've never hit a woman in my *life!*" This woman made up a complete lie. She told him that in addition to me hitting her, I also took the wheel of the car while she was driving so that she could lose control of the car.

"Pops, just listen to what you're saying. That don't even sound like me!" He wouldn't hear it. Honestly, I didn't know what to think and do. The man I looked up to, whose footsteps I chose to follow in, had chosen to believe a lie over not just the truth, but his own son.

"I think it's best for you to just get your things and get

out. I don't even look at you as my son. My son wouldn't do that." *Are you freaking kidding me?*

I could not believe that I was homeless again. After being so thrilled that my pops allowed me to come back. After praying and trusting God and thinking that my life was on the up and up. Then I had to realize that I was in a war! Satan recognized whatever value and calling that was on my life, and he was not going to sit idly by while I became who God called me to be.

My next goal was to just find somewhere to lay my head. I tried to stay with a friend that I knew when I was a teenager, but that didn't work out. We agreed that I would pay her a little bit per month, but she was using the money I was giving her to buy weed. On top of that, she told her family that I was living with her, but they told her that if I was going to be there, they wouldn't help her with her rent anymore. *Homeless again.*

My brother told me that I could sleep at the house of some 35-year-old woman that he was dating at the time. I didn't bother to pry, I just wanted to lie down. When I got there, my brother told me that I had to be gone before six a.m. the next morning. I didn't ask, I just agreed. When it came time for me to leave, I didn't have a dime on me. I asked him if I could borrow a dollar to get on the bus, and you wouldn't believe that he was reluctant! He even told me that I had to pay him back! A *dollar*. Nevermind the fact that I had let him borrow money from me before without asking for it back. I agreed to pay him back and ended up taking the bus to Walmart while I waited on the bank to open so that I could get my check.

A lot of times, we let the actions of other people or our obstacles stop us from moving forward. It all starts with our thinking; if we allow the thoughts of people control us, or if we base our moves on our current condition, we will miss the position God has for our life.

Don't let the thinking of other people imprison you from purpose. If we do that, we find ourselves questioning purpose. *Why are we going through this, or why is that happening?* In my life, I had a lot of questions that started with why, and sometimes we get to the point where we even question God with why. When I questioned God with why, he simply gave me this this answer: "Sometimes you have to just focus on the promises instead of the problem, and when you know the promises of God, you can embrace the storm."

Walking up and down the street, with nowhere to go, I found myself sleeping under a bridge for nights at a time. I had no money, and I barely ate. I never thought about going back to my father's house, I only focused on how I could bounce back. Part of me even considered seeking revenge, but I didn't allow that type of thinking to consume me. I knew that God would bring me out somehow, some way. I remember sleeping under a bridge in my work uniform and then going to the bathroom at my job to wash my face and to try to fix myself up as if nothing was wrong. I was looking bright and happy on the outside, but on the inside, there was nothing but darkness, confusion, hopelessness, and tiredness.

What type of thinking should you have when you had a good background, but in the present, you're homeless and abandoned? How do you deal with having no one there to pick up the phone to help you? On top of all of that, there is no income because you had to work a week in a hole on your job. People asked how I was able to conquer it all, and I responded that I may be crushed, but I'm crushed with a purpose.

Sometimes you gotta step out into the deep, not worrying about if you will drown, but to prove to yourself that anything is possible. Faith!

# CHAPTER 9

## *Repent, Release, Receive, and Rebuild*

SOMETIMES WE HAVE TO LOOK AT THE OBSTACLES and challenges that we face as fertilizer to our growth! Everything that we face in life, teaches us a lesson in some type of way. No matter what the situation is, there is a lesson that comes out of it. Some can make us weak and bitter in the beginning, but eventually we grow stronger. How do we overcome, and make sure that the challenges that we face don't happen again?

How do we forget the pain and the hurt of the situation? How can we forgive the situation, when it is constantly in our thoughts? The only way that we can really move on and go forth beyond what is hindering us is if we change our thinking. There are four ways to do it: repent, release, receive, and rebuild.

Repentance means to turn away and review one's actions and feelings of contrition or regret for past wrongs. It also involves a commitment to personal change and the resolve to live a more responsible life.

Repentance must start with and within us, our mind, our thinking, and God. Why is it important? Unrepentance causes bitterness. Asking for repentance is simply asking God to forgive and save us, not just from the challenges or obstacles or people that we face, but from ourselves also.

Release means to let go, to be free from bondage, and to be free from anything that's restraining us. Release simply means forgiving. Some people say forgive but never forget, but that that is not real forgiveness. If God forgave me but never forgot my sins, would I be here? In Jeremiah 31:34 God said, **"*For I will forgive their iniquity, and I will remember their sin no more.*"** When we choose to forgive others, it really benefits us more than the other person. It sets us free from those obstacles and situations that have power over us. With an unforgiving heart and mind, we will never be set free. *Free yourself!*

In my desperation to find somewhere to live, I went to a local motel and checked in. It was expensive to spend multiple nights there, and I didn't make a lot of money, but I'd pay it again to feel like I had some kind of control and covering.

I still felt defeated, and I remember calling my mom telling her that I had no idea what to do.

"Ma, it feels like every time I take one step forward, I get pushed three steps back."

My mom felt for me and sent me some money, and it seemed like as soon as she did, I ran into one of my co-workers, who was trying to leave the place where we worked.

"Aye man, I know somewhere you can work and make more money than where we're working now."

The dollar signs began to form in my eyes. "Forreal? Where?"

"It's this other restaurant that I know about. Come with me, and I'll put you on."

I went up to the restaurant that my co-worker told me about. I had on some jeans, some red and white Jordans, and a white t-shirt—definitely didn't look like I came there to ask for a job.

My boy introduced me to the manager and told him that I was interested in working there.

## Inside the Mind of a Conqueror

"I heard you were a good worker," the manager began to inquire. "What can you do?"

"I can do whatever you need me to do."

The manager gave me an apron to see what I could do. I went in the back and washed dishes, mopped the floors—I had the kitchen looking spotless. I was there for about three hours and he offered me the job on the spot. I couldn't wait to call my mom and tell her that I was about to have a second job. Just when I thought that I wanted to quit. Just when those suicidal thoughts were about to attack me again. God came to my rescue and provided for me! He showed up and reminded me that his word would never return void.

I stayed in the motel for about a month before my mom pulled some strings and got my uncle to agree to let me move in. I was so grateful. He asked me if I was working, and I told him that I had two jobs. I told him that I wouldn't be in his way, and that I would just need a place to lay my head. I told him that I could pay him and do some work around the house to help out. He only asked me for $70 a month, and I was more than happy to give that to him.

When I was experiencing living in the motel, I found myself repenting. I wasn't repenting for my actions because I didn't respond to what happen to me, but I ask God for forgiveness in my thinking. Even though I didn't react negatively in reality, my thoughts responded. I ceased all communication with my father. I even avoided going to church because I didn't want to see him. All I cared about was working and surviving. I would remember that day when I was homeless and I happened to see my father while I was lingering around Walmart with nowhere to go. He acted like nothing happened. *Didn't he know that I was on the street?* I couldn't let the anger that I had towards my dad consume me, so I began to ask God to forgive me and help me to forgive. At that point in my life and with everything that was going on, all I wanted was peace. Sometimes forgiving may help you forget your "then's", so you can be free to walk in your now."

Understand that forgiveness and moving forward may not be easy but the process is worth it. The more time we spend in this process, the stronger the healing will be. In this process, it took some time for me to get over the hurt, but I didn't allow myself to dwell on it. I began to communicate and use my time to spend with God.

**"When we become involved with God, we will evolve in him."** When I begin to focus more on God and less on my situation, I felt a burden lifted off me. It was like God gave me a second wind and the motivation I needed to go forth. He gave me the mind to receive and accept the things I couldn't change in the past, and the tools that I needed to rebuild for the present and future. Delay doesn't always means denied; I felt like this was my time to prove that I could conquer the situations and that I had the mindset of a conqueror. How do you know when you have that mindset? When you see the situation, and its presence doesn't disturb or bother you. Having the mindset of a conqueror will have you walking and moving on faith with joy and peace and motivation; it won't allow you to become distracted.

I am a living testimony. While all of this was taking place, I was still on probation—I know for a fact that it was the grace of God who kept me because if I acted on my strength and thinking, I would've failed. God began to open more doors for me—He even gave me favor with my uncle to stay in their basement. Now I know it may not be much to some people but it was better than sleeping under the bridge and wasting money staying at a motel, plus it gave me an opportunity to save my finances.

This doesn't mean that I was not on satan's hit list. Sometimes we can allow ourselves to get caught up in the good things that God has done, which is not a bad thing, but we still have to watch and pray. I think that's where I fell short. I thought I made it through, but I forgot that every level had new devils.

I remember coming home from working both jobs, and while I was going towards the basement stairs, I saw something floating across the floor. I couldn't really tell what it was, but as soon as I turned the lights on, I saw that the whole basement was flooded and all my items were submerged under water. I was shocked and aggravated at the same time because I brought it to their attention; it seemed like they didn't care. I had no clean clothes or shoes. I was thinking that my uncle would let me sleep in the living room or somewhere else dry, but all he said was, "Be careful down there."

I remember grabbing what I could and laying in the bed with tears in my eyes because I kept thinking to myself, *When will the storm be over?* How do I handle yet another challenge? What do you do when God blesses you but the enemy attacks you the very next second? How much patience will you have just when you thought it was over, but Satan stuck his hands in?

After about three days of the basement flooding, I cleaned up really good down there, and eliminated most of the mildew smell. A couple of weeks later, the basement kept flooding, so I decided to go back to the motel where I was living before. I still paid my uncle the money that I promised him, but I had to be somewhere a little safer and less hazardous to my health. Because I was working two jobs, I was able to stay at the motel for two months—staying there really didn't allow me to really save like I wanted to, but I was at least dry. I had to spend a lot more money replacing most of my clothes and shoes. Everything was ruined in that basement.

People say I could've gotten my own but in my case, it didn't work like that. Being on probation was holding me back from accomplishing and doing a lot, so I kept wondering if I really had a second chance. God begin to speak to me and told me that the things I've endure in my life, I've conquered them all. The problem was that every time I conquered one challenge, I didn't really prepare myself for what was to come. The key is that even though we are trouble on every side, if *"we look to the hills from which come our help, knowing that our help comes from God, who made the heaven and earth."* (*Psalms 121:1-2)* the key is to stay and remain focused.

# CHAPTER 10

## *Conquer What's Conquering You*

THE MOST IMPORTANT THING IN LIFE IS FINDING balance. Strength can emerge from weak moments. There are four steps that I use to conquer the obstacles in my life, and I would like to share them.

- Praying- which is asking

- Believing- which is having faith

- Moving- which is making room or space

- Receiving – being in a position to accept

Following these steps helped me realize that God has given me a second chance. A second chance to gain my life and my mind back. The second chance of thinking simply means that even though we face the challenges and battles in our life, there is always an ending to it and a beginning to something new. When we realize that we have a second change our thinking can begin to change for the better.

I remember writing down every dream and goal that I wanted to accomplish in life. I also wrote why it was important for me to accomplish these specific things. I wanted to accomplish not only the things in life in the natural, but in the spiritual also. I had to learn how to strengthen my "why" and my "how". Once my "why" was strong enough, it gave me the drive to conquer everything standing between me and my goals. When we face obstacles and situations in life, our "why" has to be greater and much stronger to take the hit. Our past experiences shouldn't hinder us but strengthen us. People always say that everything happens for a reason and a season. So, what is hindering our way to gain strength? What is stopping us from tapping into our second chance of thinking?

I remember when I was in Wednesday night bible class, we had a testimony session where everybody was sharing their testimony on how God blessed them. My pops was there, and I didn't really say anything to him. I had forgiven him for what had happened, but it was a process for me to try to intentionally form a new relationship with him. God was still working on me. I had listened to the different testimonies that the people shared, and I was moved. One thing that I know for sure is that if ever you doubt the abilities of God or feel like your situation is too much, listening to other people share how God did impossible things would surely strengthen your faith.

One of the people who stood up to give her testimony was a girl who looked like she around my age. Her name was Jaquese, and when she said that, I knew she looked familiar. I had remembered her from when we were younger—we called her Qweety back then. One thing that I could say about Qweety was that she definitely grew up. She was beautiful. As I grew in my relationship with God, I realized that I couldn't hold onto the feelings that I had for Elena. I recognized that she really didn't embody everything that I needed, God did. I didn't spend days thinking about her anymore. I wasn't still making excuses to see her or finding ways to be with her again. I cut off all communication with Elena—even changed my phone number and blocked her from my social media pages. I had the strength to walk away from the toxicity and perversion of that relationship.

Qweety was sharing how she had moved back from

California and how God blessed her to be able to work at St. John Hospital. At the end of the service, I approached her and asked if she could get me a job where she worked. I was definitely attracted to her, but I wasn't exactly in a position to be trying to bring someone else into my life. We did a little catching up and exchanged numbers.

    I texted Qweety just a friendly text saying that it was good seeing her and that I hope she was able to help me get a job where she was. I explained to her that I was working two jobs and that I wanted to let one go. I asked her if she wanted to go out to get breakfast, and we went to Coney Island right on 7 Mile and Hayes. We were just sitting there, but nobody was talking. We both were speechless, but I knew that I couldn't stop smiling. I hadn't smiled in a long time, and for some reason, I felt peace. As we were sitting there, I began to ask here questions about her life and her story.

    As much as I was interested in getting a better job, I definitely didn't want her to think that my only interest in her was her connection to the job. I asked her what made her move back to Detroit and what she'd been up to since she had been back. She told me that she moved back because she was done with school and all her friends moved out of the house that they were sharing. She asked me what I had been up to and what was going on in my life, and I got a little nervous. How do you tell someone that you went to jail for having sex with a minor? How do you tell someone who you're interested in that you wore a tether, spent the majority of your probation homeless, and that you still don't really have a stable place of residence? Women don't usually think that type of stuff is cute.

I shared with her what had been going on and what was going on now. She didn't look uncomfortable or become guarded afterwards. If anything, she seemed to be glad that things were going a lot better for me. Our food came, we ate, and as I was looking at her, I still couldn't stop smiling. It was weird that we were sitting there. I think it was because we knew each other for so long, but we never thought to go out. She dropped me off, and I told her to keep in touch, but instead I found myself texting her more.

At that time, I wasn't dating anybody because I didn't have the time to even try. I was working two jobs and I was still healing from everything I was experiencing. I didn't think it would be fair to bring Qweety into a relationship that could be toxic to her, so I didn't really pursue anything serious for a while. For some reason, I still had time to text her, and then texting turned in to calling—she was a breath of fresh air. We would be on the phone for hours.

One night, I was coming home from work, and was on the phone with Qweety. She noticed the anger in my voice. Another situation occurred, and I was at my wit's end. I told her the reason why I was angry, but while I was on the phone with her, she began to encourage me. She wanted to pray for and with me. Honestly, it was shocking because I never experienced a woman saying that she wanted to pray for me. Her prayer and her encouragement had a way of lifting me. She would send me Bible quotes and encourage me to really seek God. She challenged my faith and motivated me to really improve my relationship with God.

This had now become an ongoing thing and I found myself becoming stronger in my faith. Qweety and I would pray together all the time—we prayed about my living situation, my job situation, and whatever else was necessary to pray about. She was so dope. Sometimes in the midst of your healing process, God will connect you with people who don't mind him being in the midst. Matthew 18:20 says "Where two or three are gathered together in my name, there I am in the midst of them" (KJV). I was putting in apartment applications, and I was turned down a lot of times because of what I was on probation for. The last time that an apartment manager told me that I had been denied, I wanted to break down then and there. *I'm just trying to get back on track.*

I told Qweety all about the misfortune I was having while trying to rent an apartment, and she started helping me immediately. She arranged for me to rent out a room in her mom's house, and I was so grateful for that opportunity. I ended up moving all of my things there, and things between Qweety and me progressed quickly. We weren't so holy when we were living in her mom's house together—in fact, we started having sex.

This caused issues in my relationship with her and my relationship with God. I went back to thinking that I was the "man" again because I had two jobs making a little bit of money, had a ride-or-die woman and a stable place to live. Qweety noticed that things were going south spiritually and warned me that I shouldn't jeopardize my relationship with God. I heard her, but I was so full of myself that I even started to treat her like she was just an option in my life. She obviously wanted us to have a meaningful relationship, but I was acting like a jerk insisting that we were just friends—friends who happened to be having sex.

There was one time when she and I were sitting in the basement and I was just stuck in a trance. The T.V. was on, but I couldn't hear it. I was frozen, but tears just started to stream down my face.

"What's wrong?" Qweety frantically shouted out to me.

"I feel like something is speaking to me, but I just can't hear it."

"You should go upstairs and pray," she insisted. I started praying and I asked God to show me what he wanted me to do and how I was supposed to be living. I immediately became convicted by living with her and having sex with her. I came to Qweety, still with tears in my eyes and told her, "Babe, we're not supposed to be doing this. We're not married and we're not supposed to be having sex." I thought that she would be receptive to what I was telling her, but she figured that it was because there was someone else I was involved with. I can't blame her for thinking that way because I did act like a jerk to her for a good while.

"No, there's nobody else," I assured her. "I'm really trying to get right with God and get my life in order. This is something I feel like we need to stop doing."

I knew that it was God who was speaking and convicting me because soon after I told Qweety that we should be celibate issues started to arise with her mother. She told me that I had to leave because I shouldn't be living with Qweety and we weren't married. Qweety's mom threatened to go to our pastor and expose everything. Qweety tried to take up for me and defend me, and her mom kicked her out, too. *Homeless again.*

I wasn't too depressed about the possibility of being homeless this time because I didn't feel alone or abandoned.

It still wasn't a good feeling though. Qweety called one of her cousins to help us move our things, and he even agreed to let us stay with him. I tried to hide the tear wetting my face, but Qweety saw me and asked, "Why are you always crying."

"You don't understand," I shared. "I've been in this situation too many times, and I'm tired of it." I felt like I had brought someone else into my mess and drug her down into the pits with me. "Let's put our money together so that we can get a *home*. A place where neither of us have to worry about getting put out because somebody else is tired of us being there."

I went to work one day and Qweety called me telling me that she had used her whole check as a payment for an apartment. I thought she was lying, but when I got off work, I went to her cousin's house and she handed me the keys. We went to the apartment, and I was so relieved. "This is it!" I screamed in my head.

We were happy in our little humble abode for a while, but eventually things weren't on the up and up between us. We had got into an argument about money. Back then it was hard for me to trust another person with my money and I explained to her that because we weren't married, I shouldn't have to give her any money for anything. That was a weak rationale on my end because we were definitely living together under one roof like we were husband and wife. That argument escalated quickly, and while I was getting dressed, she called my probation officer saying that I was hitting her. *Man, come on! I'm so tired of being lied on!* I was in the background while she was on the phone asking her why she would say that I was hitting her.

I got dressed and walked outside, and I was met by two police officers who looked like they had no problem with shooting me and going out for donuts afterwards. I froze. I had no idea what was getting ready to happen. Qweety called her pops, and he came out to the building. I was on better terms with my pops, so I called him, and *he* came out to the building. It was just a big mess. I tried to convince them that it was just an argument that got out of hand, and that nothing physical had happened. That's when her father suggested that I should just leave. *Homeless again.*

I was packing my things while listening to Qweety and her pops talking and laughing like it was all a joke. *I'm not about to keep going through this. I'm not getting put out again.* I went to church after everything had deescalated. I was talking to my pops about going back with him and he basically told me that it would be best if I didn't'. I was mad but I respected where he was coming from. We would have probably been at war with each other again if I lived with him.

After church, I just started walking down Seven Mile.

Then I got an idea. *If she gonna put me out, I'm going to get all of the utilities turned off. She might put me out, but she'll be in the dark!* I was just roaming in the area for a while. I spent some time in the laundry mat until it got dark. I walked to the gas station on Chalmers and then I was approached by a guy who looked to be about my age. I was standing by the bus stop and he was asking me questions about where I came from and where I was going.

"Man, I'm just trying to find a spot where I can lay my head at."

"You look like you been going through some stuff."

"Man, that's life. I'm all good though."

He seemed like he was really cool, but something wasn't quite right about him. He kept saying that he was waiting on somebody to pick him up, but I ignored that and just asked him if I could use his phone. I called Qweety and told her that we needed to be adults and talk about our problems. She agreed and said that she would be on her way to come pick me up. I continued to talk to the guy, and we were walking up and down Chalmers until Qweety came to pick me up.

When I got in the car, Qweety had this strange look on her face.

"Um, what where you doing?"

"I was talking to that guy while I was waiting on you,"

I responded innocently but curiously because I didn't know why she would ask me that question.

"You know that's a prostitute, right?"

"Man, no he's not. We were talking and he told me that he had a spot where I could lay my head at, and we were cool. He said that somebody was going to come and pick him up."

"Wayne, listen to what you're saying."

I sat and thought for a moment and then I yelled out, "Aw *dog*! If I would have went with him I woulda been *hit*!"

That day, I decided that the streets really weren't for me, and that I needed to do whatever was necessary to bring the things in my life into their proper alignment.

# CHAPTER 11

## *Restored and Reloaded*

I CAME BACK TO OUR APARTMENT, AND AS TIME went by, Qweety and I started to get more serious about our relationship. We had been together for about two years, and at this point, everyone around us knew that we were living together—even people at our church. There was so much pressure for us to get married, but I wasn't so sure that I was ready for that. Everyone would say, "Y'all might as well do it the right way." Even though they were right, I wasn't in a race to the altar. We were just fine the way we were, and I was comfortable.

There was one particular day, I experienced some type of out of body experience. Qweety was lying in the bed, and I was lying on the floor—I had on a t-shirt and was sitting underneath the AC. It was a pretty hot day, but I was still wrapped up in a thin brown blanket. I don't know if I was dreaming or what, but as I was sleeping, I felt my ankles and my wrists getting hot. I jumped up and everything around me was pitch black. There was a bunch of smoke around me and I heard people screaming. I looked down and saw myself lying on the floor. My shirt was dirty and the people who I heard screaming were then running from some demons who were chasing them.

I looked to my left and I saw some people who were wearing jerseys, but instead of them having a team name on the front, they had the names of different demonic spirits. Some people's jerseys had "lust" and "pride" on them. I even saw some kids who had jerseys on that said "thief" and "disobedience" on them. I was looking around, and then I saw a white cloud. There was a thunderous sound coming from it, and then I saw my uncle preaching from the pulpit. I looked to my left again and saw myself and a couple of younger guys from my church ministering to some other people, but I was being whipped on my back. Then I heard a voice say, "If you don't do what I called you to do, *this* is what's going to happen to you."

After I heard that voice, I jumped up. I was back in our apartment again under the AC with my blanket on. My sudden movement must have startled Qweety because she woke up immediately and asked me what was wrong. She saw that my shirt was drenched in sweat and she asked me why I had gone into the kitchen and splashed water all over my clothes.

"I never left," I responded to her, nearly chilled white. "Why do you look so scared?" I'm sure that my fear must have frightened her, too. I explained to her all of the things that I felt and saw, and when I took off my shirt, we both saw that the back was ripped like I had been whipped. She didn't believe that I never left. She just knew that I did all of that on my own. I stopped and tried to make sense of everything that had happened, and then it clicked—*I was just in hell*. I was so shaken up that I stayed in all day.

That was a huge wake up call for me. I told my Bishop about the experience that I had, and he told me that sometimes when we ignore God for so long, he would use fear to get out attention. God had to let me know what the consequences would be for not living my life according to his will. The craziest part that I was telling my Bishop was that I had actually saw members of our church down there with me.

It was so vivid that I could name everyone that I saw. I asked my Bishop what it all meant, and he told me that those were the people that I was supposed to minister to.

After that experience, I told Qweety that we needed to line up with the word of God in *every* area of our lives. I told her that we needed to pray together more and that if we were going to be living together, we needed to be married. *We had to follow God.* We eventually got married and started to walk in what we were called to do. I told other people about that experience, not to frighten them, but to alert them that hell is real, and that goal is to be one with our Heavenly Father. Sometimes I wish I had that ripped, sweat-drenched shirt to show people who doubt that I experienced what I did. Sometimes I wish I had it as a reminder to myself, too.

My Bishop asked me if I had any more of those experiences, and thankfully, I hadn't. After Qweety and I were married, my Bishop and some of the people in my church were telling me that I should really pursue ministry so that I could touch the lives of other people. I agreed, and I started to pray for people, preach from time to time, and really share my testimony so that others could be uplifted and brought into the body of Christ.

My walk with God hasn't been easy—the enemy still tries to tempt me and cause me to fall into temptation. He still tries to conquer my thought, but I am more than a conqueror. I have dominion over him and every weapon he tries to use against me.

If I learned nothing else from all that I had been through, I learned that when we allow God to be in the midst of whatever we are going through, he will give us the strength to make it through. Only when we are one with him will begin to be victorious God has now given us the chance to conquer what's been trying to conquer us—whether it's from our past or what we might be facing now. We must move on that chance and realize that the obstacles and challenges that we face are only set up to distract us, but we can't let them stop us.

This reminds me of the story of David and Goliath. Goliath was a giant in who was defeated by David. How did David defeat him? He used a mere slingshot and a stone to knock Goliath down and then David grabbed Goliath's sword and cut off his head. Notice the steps that David took to conquer what was trying to conquer him: he killed goliath with a rock, he then stole Goliath's sword and destroyed him by cutting off his head. That's what we have to do to Satan and his kingdom and to the things that's conquering us. We have to kill those things with a rock which is Jesus Christ, steal its power with the sword, the Word of God, and destroying its head with our praise.

## Inside the Mind of a Conqueror

Jesus Christ, himself, had some things that he also had to conquer. If we read Matthew 4:1-11, it talks about how Jesus was led by the spirit into the wilderness to be tempted by Satan. Realize that the devil knows the word of God, too. Sometimes he will prevent the word and use his twisted words to try to conquer you too, Satan even offered Jesus the kingdoms of the world just to get Jesus to bow down to him. Because Jesus had fasted and prayed, he was able to conquer temptation. Even in the garden while he was praying, he was sorrowful because he knew it was his time to go to the cross. The bible says that he prayed so hard that he begun to sweat and his sweat was like drops of blood (Matthew 26:36-56).

As Jesus continued praying the Bible says that God sent an angel to strengthen him. Whenever we take the time out to fast and pray, God will send angels to give us strength. Strength in our thinking, physical strength, and spiritual strength.

When I think about all of the things that tried to conquer me and kill me spiritually and physically, I am reminded of the story of Lazarus. When he was sick, his sister went to Jesus to ask if he can come and lay his hands on Lazarus. By the time Jesus got to him, he had died and been placed in a tomb. One thing I noticed about this story was that there was a man in a dead situation who was trapped in darkness. Sometimes while we are dead in the challenges that we face, and dead in our situations, God doesn't have to lay his hands on us to bring us back to life. He doesn't have to physically touch us to bring us out of darkness.

If we look closely at the story of Lazarus, he was raised from the dead and came forth out of darkness because Jesus spoke to him. That's why it's important to have an open and clear mind because when God speaks, you need to be able to respond to what he is saying. Even though I was in a dark place, God spoke to me and the stone door of depression, low self-esteem, mental imprisonment, ungodly soul-ties, and suicide have now rolled away. I am a conqueror because I had decided that nothing is more important than my relationship with God and that when the attacks of the enemy come against me, I have a God who has given me everything to be a conqueror.

J. Oswald Sanders said, "Before we can conquer the world, we must first conquer the self." Before I left, I went into my bishop's office and I began sharing my story and all of the challenges that I faced. He said something that stuck with me until this day: for every problem you face, there is a promise that is fulfilled. I remember walking to my uncle's house, thinking about all that I'd been through and I realized that my second chance was God's grace. It was his grace that

## Inside the Mind of a Conqueror

kept me, and grounded me. Even when I fell short, his grace sustained me. I understood then and I understand now that no matter what comes my way, no matter what the challenges or obstacles may be, I can conquer them all in my mind. I got a second chance because of God's Grace. When you understand who and where you were, you can appreciate who you are and where you're going. When you conquer the attacks of the enemy in your mind, you'll win in reality because it's in you to finish— God had predestined you to finish. When we think in our minds that we are victorious, we'll know that we are victorious and then we will become Victorious.

I challenge you to ignite and stir up the conqueror on the inside of you. Chant these words daily as a reminder of who you are and you will conquer what's conquering you:

**I am the head and not the tail!**
**I am above and not beneath!**
**I am strong!**
**I am an overcomer!**
**Because you died for me Jesus:**
**I am free!**
**I am healed!**
**I am delivered!**

Wayne Billy, Jr.

I will win!

I will not be defeated!

It's in me to finish!

I am and always will be a *conqueror!*

*I can do all things through Christ which strengthened me.*

*Philippians 4:13 (KJV)*

# About the Author

**Wayne Billy, Jr.** is a Detroit native and product of the Detroit Public School System. Serving as a minister at Jesus Tabernacle of Deliverance Ministries under the pastoral guidance of Bishop David Billy, Sr., Billy officially obtained his ministerial license in 2014 and has been fervently spreading the Gospel of Jesus Christ ever since. Wayne Billy, Jr. is a devoted husband, father, minister, and author. He currently resides in Detroit, MI with his two children and his wife, Jaquese Billy.

www.ingramcontent.com/pod-product-compliance
Lightning Source LLC
Chambersburg PA
CBHW051804040426
42446CB00007B/517